The Channel Islands

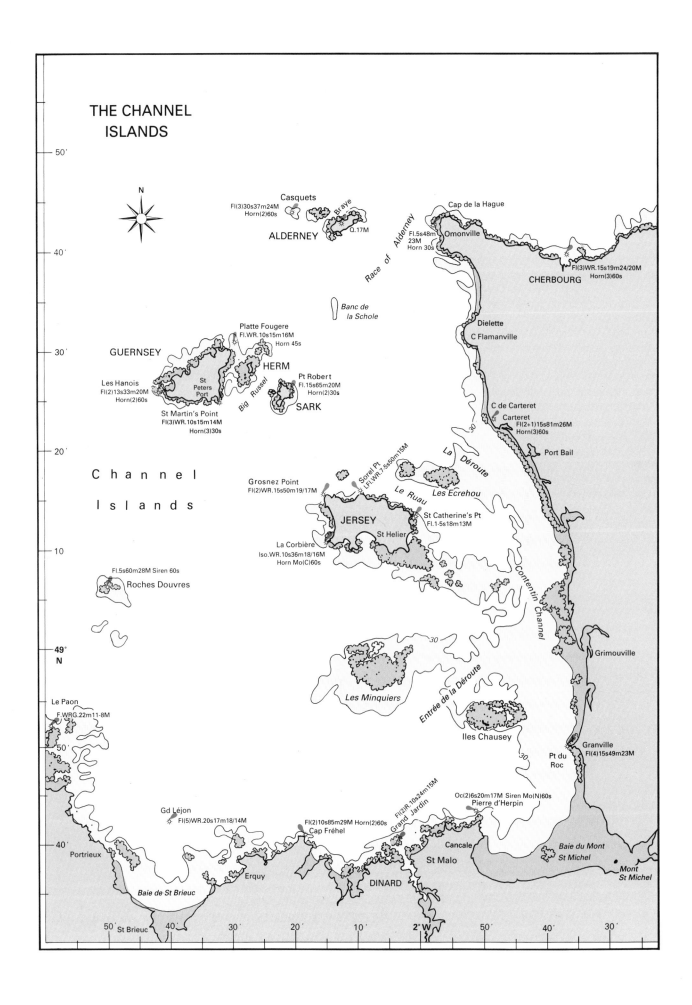

THE CHANNEL
ISLANDS

N

Casquets
Fl(3)30s37m24M
Horn(2)60s

Braye

ALDERNEY

Q.17M

Cap de la Hague

Omonville

Fl.5s48m
23M
Horn 30s

Race of Alderney

Fl(3)WR.15s19m24/20M
Horn(3)60s

CHERBOURG

Banc de
la Schole

Dielette

C Flamanville

Platte Fougere
Fl.WR.10s15m16M

Horn 45s

GUERNSEY

HERM

Les Hanois
Fl(2)13s33m20M
Horn(2)60s

St
Peters
Port

Big Russel

Pt Robert
Fl.15s65m20M
Horn(2)30s

C de Carteret

Carteret
Fl(2+1)15s81m26M
Horn(3)60s

St Martin's Point
Fl(3)WR.10s15m14M
Horn(3)30s

SARK

Port Bail

C h a n n e l

I s l a n d s

Grosnez Point
Fl(2)WR.15s50m19/17M

Sorel Pt
Lfl.WR.7.5s50m15M

La Déroute

Le Ruau

Les Ecrehou

St Catherine's Pt
Fl.1.5s18m13M

JERSEY

St Helier

La Corbière
Iso.WR.10s36m18/16M
Horn Mo(C)60s

Grimouville

Fl.5s60m28M Siren 60s

Roches Douvres

Contentin Channel

30

49°
N

Les Minquiers

Entrée de la Déroute

Le Paon
F.WRG.22m11-8M

Iles Chausey

Granville
Fl(4)15s49m23M

50'

Pt du
Roc

Oc(2)6s20m17M Siren Mo(N)60s
Pierre d'Herpin

Baie du Mont
St Michel

Gd Léjon
Fl(5)WR.20s17m18/14M

Fl(2)R.10s24m15M

Grand Jardin

Fl(2)10s85m29M Horn(2)60s
Cap Fréhel

Cancale

Mont
St Michel

Portrieux

St Malo

Erquy

DINARD

Baie de St Brieuc

50' St Brieuc   40'   30'   20'   10'   2° W   50'   40'   30'

The Channel Islands

**ROYAL CRUISING CLUB
PILOTAGE
FOUNDATION**

Compiled by Nick Heath

Imray Laurie Norie & Wilson Ltd
St Ives Cambridgeshire England

Published by
Imray Laurie Norie & Wilson Ltd
Wych House, St Ives, Huntingdon
Cambridgeshire PE17 4BT England
☎ +44 (0)1480 462114 *Fax* +44 (0)1480 496109
E-mail editor@imray.com
1997

ISBN 0 85288 361 7

British Library Cataloguing in Publication Data
A catalogue record for this title is available from the British Library.

CAUTION
Every effort has been made to ensure the accuracy of this book. It contains selected information and thus is not definitive and does not include all known information on the subject in hand; this is particularly relevant to the plans, which should not be used for navigation. The Pilotage Foundation believes that its selection is a useful aid to prudent navigation, but the safety of a vessel depends ultimately on the judgement of the navigator, who should assess all information, published or unpublished.

PLANS
The plans in this guide are not to be used for navigation. They are designed to support the text and should always be used with navigational charts.

All bearings are from seaward and refer to true north. Symbols are based on those used by the British Admiralty – users are referred to *Symbols and Abbreviations (NP 5011)*.

CORRECTIONS
The editor would be glad to receive any corrections, information or suggestions which readers may consider would improve the book, as new impressions will be required from time to time. Letters should be addressed to the Editor, *The Channel Islands*, care of the publishers. The more precise the information the better, but even partial or doubtful information is helpful, if it is made clear what the doubts are.

CORRECTIONAL SUPPLEMENTS
Imray pilot books are amended at intervals by the issue of correctional supplements. Supplements, if available, are supplied free of charge with the books when they are purchased. Further supplements are available from the publishers. The following should be quoted:

1. Name of book
2. Date of edition (above)
3. Date of last supplement (if applicable)
4. Name and address to which supplement should be sent on a stamped addressed A4 envelope.

The last input of technical information was February 1997.

Printed in Great Britain by Bath Press Colour Books Ltd, Blantyre, Scotland.

Contents

Foreword

The Royal Cruising Club Pilotage Foundation, a registered charity, is based on a very generous benefaction by an American member of the Royal Cruising Club, Dr Fred Ellis, and has been established to encourage the aspiring sailor to extend his cruising range with confidence. It edits and updates existing pilot books and guides and initiates its own where a need is recognised.

The Foundation is privileged that Malcolm Robson gave to it the copyright of all his pilot books, coupled with the request that the books should be revised as needed. The Foundation is most grateful to Nick Heath who so manfully undertook the task of revising the volume on the Channel Islands but, as he mentions in his acknowledgements below, this volume has to be the successor to Malcolm Robson's work, rather than a revision. Malcolm Robson was a member of the Royal Cruising Club and, with his death, the Foundation sadly lost his skill in drawing. It proved impossible to keep the book up to date in his style and so it was decided that the best option was to produce a new book. However, the Foundation wishes to pay tribute to Malcolm Robson and it is my pleasant duty to dedicate this new pilot to his memory. His knowledge of the Islands and his work on his own pilot were of great help to the Foundation in the production of this volume.

W.H Batten Chairman
Royal Cruising Club
Pilotage Foundation
1997

Also by the Royal Cruising Club Pilotage Foundation

North Brittany
North Biscay
Atlantic Islands
Atlantic Spain and Portugal
North Africa
The Baltic Sea
Faeroe, Iceland and Greenland
Lesser Antilles (with SHOM)
Atlantic Crossing Guide (A&C Black Ltd)
Pacific Crossing Guide (A&C Black Ltd)
South Atlantic Coast of South America (RCC)

Acknowledgements

The RCC was honoured when the late Malcolm Robson invited the Pilotage Foundation to maintain the tradition of providing a pilot book specifically for the Channel Islands.

When the editor made a preliminary visit in January 1994, he met with an enthusiastic response from local yachtsmen and professional seamen who offered to assist, advising that a new book rather than a new edition should be compiled to replace Malcolm's pilot.

As a result of their help the editor can feel that in many ways he is indeed editor rather than author of this book.

Among the many who assisted, the following require special mention and thanks.

Alderney The Braye harbour staff, Steve Shaw (harbourmaster, lifeboat coxswain and pilot); Bryan Markell (air traffic controller, expert on the inshore passages and fisherman); David McAllister (fisherman); Roland Neal of Mainbrayce and the harbour staff.

Guernsey Derek Boyer, for providing air transport, accommodation and a boat; Jean-Pierre Sidaner for many introductions and acting coxswain; Bob Morey (senior St Peter Port pilot) and Barry Paint (St Sampson pilot) for showing me the transits; Dick Sherwill for showing me the passages round Herm and Sark and John Frankland, David Nicolle, Robert Sample and John Torode for providing advice, tidal information and photographs.

Sark Miss C. Bell (chairwoman of Sark Pilotage Committee) and Dick Adams for advice, tidal information and photographs.

Jersey Members of the St Helier Yacht Club and the Royal Channel Islands Yacht Club in Jersey and Guernsey. Roger Thébault for the section on weather; Bob Lawrence for making introductions; Michael Allo RCC for accommodation on his boat; Frank Lawrence for photographs of Les Minquiers; Nicholas Bailhache RCC for much information and a visit to Les Minquiers; Blair Sarre for visits to Les Ecrehou where he has a hut; David Coom for a visit to Les Minquiers, where his brother has a hut and for taking me through the Gutters; Peter Warren and Tony Clarke for showing me many transits and a passage through the Gutters and Mike Backhurst for photographs and advice.

Peter Carnegie RCC deserves special thanks for flying me round the islands for photography and later for flying friends to take more photos under improved conditions.

N.E. Heath
February 1997

Introduction

Why is a Channel Islands pilot book necessary?

Some yachts never visit the Channel Islands because their owners are discouraged by stories of the large tidal range and strong streams. A second category of yachts are seen making a brief stop in Braye, St Peter Port or St Helier when on passage to the Brittany coast, and a third category are used by weekenders who have little time to explore.

If the owners of yachts in the first category make careful preparation by reading this pilot book, consulting tide tables and charts and carefully monitoring the weather forecasts, they will find their first visit to be an interesting and rewarding experience which should encourage them to return, with time to spare for further exploration.

With a young family on board, the editor was in the second category and, when sailing from the Solent, with the necessity for short passages, would call at Cherbourg and Alderney and spend a few days at St Peter Port, for bathing and a visit to the Butterfly Farm or other places of interest to the young, before proceeding to the Brittany coast. As they grew older, we would spend more days exploring Herm and Sark and then continue on to Jersey.

Alderney is the obvious primary target for weekenders and later, with a series of long weekends, coupled with reliable weather forecasts, the first stop could be St Peter Port, to clear customs, and then there would be time for a look at Sark or Herm or, in settled weather, some of the Guernsey anchorages.

These visits will provide experience as well as respect for the tides and it will be seen that they are there to be used to become an aid rather than a threat to an extended summer cruise.

Formalities

The island of Jersey and the Bailiwick of Guernsey (consisting of Alderney, Guernsey, Herm and Sark) have separate customs regulations, and visiting yachts must arrive at a port of entry flying the 'Q' flag and clear customs.

The ports of entry are as follows:
Alderney Braye
Guernsey, Herm and Sark St Peter Port or Beaucette Marina
Jersey St Helier or Gorey. Les Minquiers and Les Ecrehou are controlled by Jersey.

A yacht passing between Jersey and Guernsey (with Herm and Sark) or Alderney must clear customs on arrival at the new port.

Fuel and facilities

The islands are VAT free and both diesel and petrol are cheaper than on the 'mainland' and much cheaper than in France.

However, due to the cost of transport, the prices in the shops are not significantly below those on the mainland.

Moorings, marinas and yacht clubs in the major ports

Alderney

Moorings are available in Braye Harbour and the yacht club welcomes visitors. Fuel in the inner harbour, showers and toilets on the quay.

Guernsey

Berths, fuel and the usual marina facilities are available at St Peter Port and Beaucette Marina. The Royal Channel Islands Yacht Club and the Guernsey Yacht Club welcome visitors.

Jersey

At the time of writing there are two marinas with all facilities in St Helier, and there will shortly be three. Fuel nearby the St Helier Yacht Club, which welcomes visitors. The Royal Channel Islands Yacht Club is situated at St Aubin.

Gorey is the second port of entry, providing drying moorings, fuel and toilets.

Safety

There is no coastguard as such in the Channel Islands. However, the harbourmasters' offices in Jersey, Guernsey and Alderney undertake coastguard duties through the radio stations.

Jersey is a Marine Coast Radio Station issuing navigational warnings and weather reports.

Jersey, Guernsey and Alderney have VHF, VHF direction finding and radar assistance (VTS) on request.

Between Easter and the end of September Alderney Radio operates from 0800–1700 seven days a week. During the winter months it operates from 0800–0700 Monday to Thursday, 0800–1500

Friday and is closed at weekends.

In an emergency, when closed call Jersey Radio, CROSSMA (French Coastguard) or St Peter Port Radio. Alderney Radio can then be operational within a few minutes.

Jersey Radio is equipped with the full GMDSS and Safety System, with VHF using DSC on Ch 70. On the European coastline, radio stations are similarly equipped and the system will be installed along the S coast of the UK by September 1997.

Weather

This section has been provided by Mr R. E. Thébault, a keen yachtsman and Principal of the Jersey Meteorological Department which is responsible for providing forecasts for the Channel Islands.

The Channel Islands share the rather changeable maritime climate of the rest of the British Isles but with some important differences. These differences are partly because of the more southerly location of the Islands and partly because of the proximity to France, with Brittany in particular, providing considerable shelter from moist southwesterly winds which prevail at certain times of the year.

The position of the Channel Islands off north France is shown in Figure 1, page 4.

This section will deal with the singularities of the Channel Islands weather and the local effects. Of necessity, weather features such as anticyclones, depressions, fronts and airstreams will be mentioned but the reader is referred to other publications for an explanation of these.

The variable nature of the weather is such that all wind directions are experienced with a significant frequency in the Channel Islands, although winds from the west and WNW are the most frequent, followed by winds from the northeast and east. The latter directions are particularly prevalent during the spring.

The mean wind speed in the Channel Islands varies from around 12 knots in the south to 14 knots in the north – force 4 – which is an ideal wind for sailing but does mean that the significant wave heights are around 3–4ft (1m) on average.

This is in the slight to moderate category of sea state and, locally, the seas can be much rougher than this where strong tidal currents flow against the wind. In all except light wind conditions therefore, crossings should be made during the period when the wind is with the tide if at all possible.

CHARACTER OF THE WINDS

Winds from the northwest quadrant

More often than not, northwesterly winds are associated with polar maritime airstreams. The visibility is generally good but, in unstable situations, it will be reduced by showers which can also be quite squally. In anticyclonic conditions the weather is normally clear and fine.

Cumulus clouds form over the Islands and over the French coast, and in these conditions I have often been able to locate the positions of Jersey and Guernsey from the 'Island brew' cumulus cloud while on passage between French ports.

Occasionally, airstreams of tropical maritime origin flow into the area on northwesterly winds, having come up from tropical regions behind a warm front, moving around a ridge just to the west of the British Isles.

In these situations the visibility can be poor with drizzle and fog but it is unusual for the fog to be persistent, and frequently it lifts off the sea surface a little allowing moderate visibility at sea level while the tops of the Islands remain in fog. As the wind backs towards the west, fog becomes more of a problem.

The shape of the French coastline around the Channel Islands has an important effect on a northwesterly wind. The long stretch of north to south coastline of the Normandy Cotentin between Cap de la Hague and Granville, together with the Brittany coast between Ile de Bréhat and St Malo form an ideal funnel into which northwesterly winds are accelerated.

The effect can result in some very unpleasant seas and a pressure gradient which would normally produce say a force 5 can result in conditions more typical of force 6 or 7 and correspondingly much rougher seas. Strong tidal currents flowing against the northwesterly wind can further worsen the situation.

The worst conditions occur during the ebb tide, where strong currents flow towards the northwest. These are shown in figure 2 and include:

a. The strip of sea off the Cotentin, up to 15M offshore and especially the area between Jersey and Les Ecrehou.

b. Most of the sea area south and southwest of Jersey, including the stretch of water off the Brittany coast between St Malo to Cap Fréhel and right up to Ile de Bréhat.

I have a very clear recollection of one occasion, on passage from Granville to St Helier during a spring tide, when it took over 2 hours compared to the normal 30 minutes to travel the 12 nautical miles between the northeast corner of Chausey and the northeast Minquiers buoy. The wind was a force 5 in a pressure pattern which only merited a force 4 but the sea was rough with steep breaking waves continually crashing onto the bow of the boat.

Winds from the southwest quadrant

Southwesterly winds are generally mild and moist and fog is a frequent problem, particularly in spring and early summer, when the sea temperature in the Channel is relatively low compared to the air temperature. In cyclonic conditions these air streams also bring thick drizzle, while in anticyclonic situations the fog is often patchy with the sun breaking through at times.

Shelter from Brittany is a major consideration

with winds from the southwest quarter. The map in figure 3 shows how the further south one goes the greater the shelter received from the Brittany land mass which rises to almost 1000ft (300m) above sea level in the centre. Passage across the land tends to dry out the airstream and so disperse any fog, while friction over the land reduces the wind speed.

With a westerly wind, the only relatively large area of sea which is sheltered is in the bay of Saint Brieuc and more especially along the stretch of coast between Paimpol and Dahouet. However, as the wind backs, the area south of Jersey becomes increasingly sheltered by Brittany and, for example, with a 250° wind direction, on a journey southward from St Helier one will go from a comparatively exposed situation to an airstream which has passed over the 70 nautical miles of land between Brest and Paimpol. In these situations it is not unusual to commence the journey from St Helier in dull weather with drizzle and fog and a fresh WSW wind, then to pass into much more pleasant conditions with sunshine, good visibility and less wind only some 8–12M south of Jersey.

For Jersey to be sheltered by Brittany the general wind flow needs to back to about 235°, while Guernsey does not benefit from much shelter until the wind is back to 220°. In summer, the contrast in the weather between the exposed north and the sheltered south of the area is at its greatest and it is not unusual for the wind to fall light in the zone sheltered from the southwest. If it becomes very hot inland over France, onshore sea breezes can develop in the afternoon from Granville, all along the coast to Ile de Bréhat, with light north or northeasterly winds blowing onshore for a time against the general southwesterly flow which only re-establishes itself late in the night.

In southwesterly wind situations, wave heights in the south of the area are generally much lower than in the north. This is because of the double effect of lighter winds in the shelter of Brittany and the shorter fetch over which the wind can act to produce waves. North of the sheltered zone winds are stronger and the fetch can be unlimited so that the sea state becomes much rougher.

Tidal currents flowing against the wind – that is flowing towards the southwest – will make the seas even rougher. The Alderney Race, the Great Russel and the area generally around Sark can produce some exceptionally rough conditions when southwesterly winds blow against the tide, particularly where strong overfalls occur in association with shallow banks. These areas are shown on figure 4.

The roughest seas occur around Alderney and Cap de la Hague but conditions can be particularly bad west of Guernsey, at the southern end of the Little Russel and in the Great Russel, all just after LW St Helier and for the first three hours of the flood tide.

Off the northwest corner of Jersey, conditions can be unpleasant during the last two hours of the ebb tide. The short stretch of water along Jersey's south coast between Noirmont and Corbière is to be avoided in strong winds when the direction is from between west and southwest and even from the WNW. A combination of shallows and strong tidal currents causes the swell and wind waves to build up during the period of the ebb tide to give some very unpleasant conditions, with steep confused waves, giving a generally very rough sea state.

Winds from the southeast quadrant

Winds from this direction are the least frequent, but nevertheless occur on average each year for about 19% of the time.

In settled weather the airflow normally has a long landtrack across Europe and it is dry and hazy with only moderate visibility. In winter it is cold and winds can be quite strong.

In summer these airstreams are warm and can produce some of the finest weather the Islands enjoy. Daytime heating over France often causes the winds over the whole of the Channel Islands area to fall light during the afternoon. However, an exception to this can occur when a heat low develops over France. With ESE winds the airflow backs to the northeast as the low develops and the wind increases as the day progresses and is most noticeable in the late afternoon and evening.

In hot weather, thunderstorms can break out over France and drift up across the sea, often arriving over the Islands at night, but their development can usually be anticipated by the formation of alto-cumulus castellanus during daytime.

A spell of southeasterly winds can also occur in the circulation of a stationary depression centred over Biscay. In these situations the airstream flows in from the Atlantic over Biscay and then over France. The visibility is normally good but thunderstorms and showers are relatively frequent. The classical large cumulus and cumulonimbus clouds can be seen in the distance, forming over France during the day. They drift up to affect the Islands in the late afternoon and evening.

In quiet anticyclonic conditions, radiation fog often forms over France at night and drifts up on the southeasterly winds to affect the Islands. The worst areas of fog formation are the low-lying land south of Mont Saint Michel and the river valleys.

It is not unusual for ribbons of fog with a top of about 300ft (100m) above sea level, to flow out from the estuaries. I have known patchy fog from the Rance estuary to reach Jersey in the late morning some hours after the visibility had improved in the estuary itself around St Malo.

Sometimes, mainly in autumn and winter, much more extensive fog can form over a large part of the French land mass, and when this occurs it can extend over the whole of the Channel Islands area and persist for long periods.

I am not aware of any local effects on the sea worthy of note with southeasterly winds, except that even with a moderate to fresh breeze, a nasty short, choppy sea will develop quickly, particularly where the wind blows against the tide.

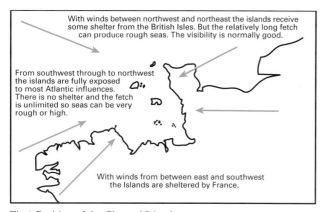

With winds between northwest and northeast the islands receive some shelter from the British Isles. But the relatively long fetch can produce rough seas. The visibility is normally good.

From southwest through to northwest the islands are fully exposed to most Atlantic influences. There is no shelter and the fetch is unlimited so seas can be very rough or high.

With winds from between east and southwest the Islands are sheltered by France.

Fig 1 Position of the Channel Islands
and the main wind/sea effects

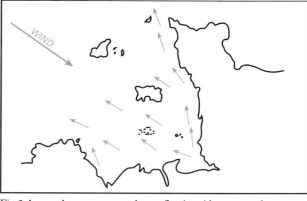

Fig 2 Areas where strong northwest flowing tides can produce
very rough seas in northwesterly wind situations.

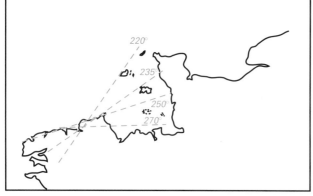

Fig 3 Lines to the south of which there is substantial
shelter from Brittany from given wind directions.

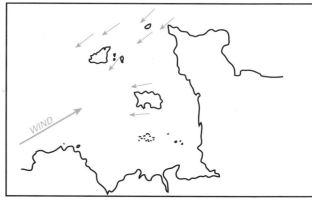

Fig 4 Areas where strong flowing tides produce very
rough seas in southwesterly wind situations.

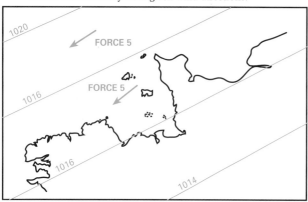

Fig 5a Typical isobaric situation and winds with
a northeasterly in the early morning.

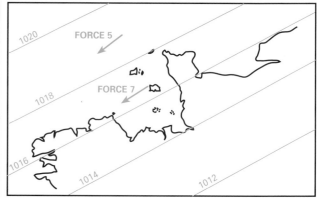

Fig 5b Typical isobaric situation and winds in
the afternoon after heating over France.

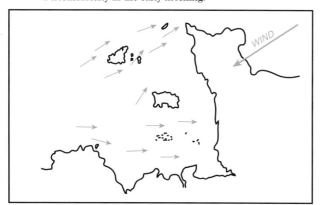

Fig 6 Areas where strong flowing tides can produce very
rough seas in northeasterly wind situations.

The stretch of water between Ile de Bréhat and Roches Douvres experiences the worst conditions but the southern end of the Little Russel can also produce some nasty conditions, particularly around the time of low water.

Winds from the northeast quadrant

Northeasterly winds in the Channel Islands area are normally associated with fine, dry, hazy weather. The most common pressure pattern is a belt of high pressure extending from the British Isles to Scandinavia and low pressure over Europe. This situation is most likely to occur during the spring.

The long track over northern Europe, which includes some very industrial areas, fills the air with dust and smoke particles, so this is always a very hazy airstream with visibility typically in the range of 2–5M. An exception occurs when an anticyclone is centred over the British Isles, with the airstream flowing down the North Sea and curving around through the straits of Dover to give a northeasterly flow down the English Channel, in which case the visibility is normally good but with cloud and even showers forming due to the long sea track.

Northeasterly winds are the most fickle to affect the Channel Islands area. The air seems to cling to the land surface so that it is difficult to find shelter from the wind. On a number of occasions I have taken my boat into Portelet on Jersey's southwest coast and also Havre Gosselin on the west coast of Sark, looking for shelter from a force 4–5 northeasterly so that my family could enjoy a spot of sunbathing out of the wind, only to find strong gusts blowing down the cliffs and making conditions unpleasant. Yet both bays are well sheltered from the northeast by high cliffs.

Northeasterly winds tend to hug the west coast of Guernsey, adding to the difficulties of navigating close inshore along a hazardous coastline.

In fine weather, the northeasterly often manifests strong diurnal variations, with the highest winds occurring in the late afternoon and early evening. I attribute this effect to heating over France and the shape of the French coastline. This can best be understood by reference to figure 5a which shows an isobaric pattern for a typically northeasterly airflow. The spacing of the isobars shown would give a northeasterly wind of say, force 5. Let this be the situation early one morning in May or June on a sunny day. As the day progresses, the land mass of France will warm up considerably and the heating will cause a fall of pressure inland. A pressure fall of between 2 and 4 millibars due to heating is not unusual at this time of year. However, the temperature over the sea does not change much so there is no corresponding fall of pressure over the English Channel.

Assuming that no other changes are taking place, heating over France will produce the pattern shown on figure 5b. It can be seen that the pressure gradient has increased over the Channel Islands area and along the length of the French coast. It is not unusual for a force 5 in the morning to increase to force 7 in the late afternoon and evening because of daytime heating over France.

In practice the situation is more complex and on some occasions the diurnal increase in wind gradually extends northwards to cover the whole of the Channel Islands area while at other times it is limited to a narrow band only about 12M wide. The area around Chausey often enjoys calmer conditions with the edge of the strong winds lying to the north somewhere between Chausey and Jersey.

Above about 15 knots – that's the top of a force 4 a northeasterly produces a nasty short choppy sea generally over the Channel Islands area with the worst conditions associated with wind against tide, as might be expected. Around Guernsey and Alderney this is between one hour before and two hours after high water. It is very noticeable at the northern end of the Little Russel, where a 5 knot spring tide will produce some quite vicious overfalls.

Undoubtedly, the worst conditions occur in the Alderney Race. Travelling north to pass between Alderney and Cap de la Hague, with a wind from the northeast force 3 to 4, conditions can change from a slight to moderate choppy sea to a situation where one is faced with a wall of water as the Race is entered. This is followed by a stretch of very rough sea with steep standing waves.

South of Jersey the worst conditions occur during the four hours leading up to high water St Helier. The areas where wind against tide effects are strongest are shown on figure 6.

Fetch is also important and wave heights increase considerably north of the shelter zone provided by the Cotentin. Reference to figure 6 will show that the fetch changes from about 40M or less to well over 100M north of the line lying approximately from Guernsey to Cap de la Hague. This is another reason why conditions in the Alderney Race can be exceptionally rough and clearly this area should be avoided in all but ideal conditions.

UNDERSTANDING WEATHER OBSERVATIONS IN THE CHANNEL ISLANDS

Many weather bulletins for shipping contain lists of observations or reports of actual weather, from stations in the area, and the Channel Islands are no exception. However, in order to use this information fully it is necessary to understand the nature of the data contained and to know how representative the individual station observations are in comparison to conditions in the open sea.

Dealing firstly with the information in the reports; this usually consists of time of report, wind direction and force, visibility, weather, pressure and pressure tendency. Taking each of these in turn:

Time It is important to remember that the observation is a statement of conditions at a given time, or in the case of wind and pressure tendency for a specific period prior to the time of observation. Any events or changes which occur outside of the time of observation are not reported.

Wind direction Airflow is often very turbulent with many short-term fluctuations. The average or mean wind direction for the 10 minute period prior to the time of observations is therefore used. The direction is given in degrees from true north, or as a compass point, and it is the direction *from* which the wind is blowing which is stated. This is, of course, the opposite to the convention used to describe a bearing or a course *to* a destination.

Wind speed or wind force Like the wind direction, the wind speed is irregular and consists of gusts and lulls lasting only a matter of seconds, so again the wind speed is taken as the mean over the 10-minute period immediately prior to the time of observation. The gusts or peak speeds are reported, in addition to the mean speed, only when they exceed the mean speed by 10 knots or more.

Nowadays, at many meteorological observing stations the 10-minute mean wind speed is calculated by computer and this gives a much more accurate reading than can be obtained by other methods such as watching a dial, which more often than not produces an overestimate.

Visibility The visibility reported by meteorological stations is always the lowest visibility observed, taking account of all directions. To use an extreme example, if the visibility is only 300m to the north because of a fog patch but is 20M in other directions, the visibility is reported as 300m.

Weather This is reserved for describing the significant weather at the time of observation, such as rain, drizzle, fog etc. If there is no significant weather, the state of the sky is described using the terms fine, fair (partly cloudy) or cloudy.

Pressure The pressure at the time of observation, calculated to mean sea level is given in millibars (now officially called hectopascals).

Pressure tendency The overall change during the past three hours is described.

LOCATION OF STATIONS

Topography can exert a large influence on the local weather and particularly on the wind. A headland, a hill and even a pier or breakwater constitutes a barrier to the airflow. The wind is increased, often very considerably, around the sides and along the top of such obstructions, while there is normally an appreciable decrease in wind speed behind the obstruction.

Inland, many features such as buildings, hedgerows and trees have the effect of slowing down the airflow generally, so that wind speeds inland are less than those over the open water, given the same pressure situation.

Unfortunately not all observing sites are well situated. Stations located on headlands or hills will give excessively high readings in some wind directions while with other directions the same stations can give misleadingly low readings.

There is a danger here that the inexperienced sailor can be misled by weather observations and he or she must learn the wind directions from which the various reporting stations in the area receive shelter and will therefore under read. Knowledge of those stations which over read is perhaps even more important since he or she may imagine that a force 6 has been easily coped with, when in fact the wind experienced was 1 or 2 forces less!

The weather reports for Granville provide a good example of the effect of topography. The station is situated on the promontory called Pointe du Roc, which juts out from the coastline towards the west. With winds blowing from the south and the north the airflow is increased around this headland and is often 1 or 2 forces on the Beaufort Scale higher than out to sea.

With winds from the west the readings are representative of conditions offshore, while with easterly winds the station is well sheltered and will read considerably less compared with offshore.

Similar effects can be found around Jersey; the reports given by the Corbière radiobeacon on the southwest corner of the island will often give high readings compared to over the open sea – with wind directions from south to southeast and with those between north and northwest.

Dinard and Cherbourg airports experience some shelter especially with winds from the southerly point and consequently in these situations both stations will under read compared with conditions at sea.

Topography also affects wind direction and in particular the air will flow around obstructions. To use a Jersey example, a westerly wind will locally be from the southwest at La Rocque and from the northwest off Rozel. Even more important, a strong southwesterly wind will flow around the southeast corner of the island and blow into Gorey, with little reduction in strength.

Around Sark it is difficult to find shelter with a wind of more than force 4, regardless of direction. The same applies to the south coast of Guernsey, where a breezy northerly flow can produce some unpleasant and unpredictable wind eddies down into the bays.

Observations of visibility can also vary with location and topography. It goes without saying that the visibility in a fog patch will be very poor, but may be in the very good category not far away, outside the fog. Height above sea level is often a cause of apparent discrepancies between observations at coastal stations and conditions at sea, since with low cloud a station 200–300ft (100m) above sea level may be experiencing poor visibility, while conditions at sea level, below the cloud, are much better. However, when cloud is very low it does not take much of a change to bring the base down to sea level, with a consequent deterioration in visibility.

It can therefore be said that observations from reporting stations do give a useful indication of the conditions which existed in the area at the time of observations, but they always need to be interpreted with local knowledge. It is important to draw a clear distinction between the observations and the forecast. The latter being a general description of the weather expected in the future during the period stated.

SEA STATE

A section on weather observations aimed at mariners would be incomplete without a mention of sea state. Human estimates of wave height are often unreliable because of the very confused nature of waves, and very few actual measurements of wave height are taken.

In the Channel Islands area the Channel light vessel (49°55'·4N 2°53'·7W) has a wave sensor and reports the period and height of the waves regularly with each observation. A small wave-rider buoy is deployed to the south of Jersey for periods of up to nine months at a time and this provides invaluable information on wave conditions locally.

As already mentioned, wave heights can vary considerably, so a sample over a period of at least 10 minutes is normally taken. However, with wave heights, a simple arithmetic mean over the whole range of the sample is not used (as it is with wind speed and direction). Instead, the mean of the highest one third of the waves is used to describe the sea state. This is called *the significant wave height.* Normally the highest wave measured in a 10-minute period is about 1½ times the significant wave height. However, in certain situations it can be more than this especially when swell is present.

The wave height is the *total height* from the *top of the crest* to the *bottom of the trough.*

When the wind strength is below a force 4, the waves produced by the wind generally cause no problems. However, the range of sea state generated by winds between force 4 and 6 is very large and extends from conditions which are manageable for all but the smallest craft, and comfortable for most, at the bottom of force 4, to conditions at the top end of force 6 which are very uncomfortable, frightening and even dangerous for many vessels.

ACKNOWLEDGEMENT

I would like to thank Tim Lillington, meteorological observer at Guernsey airport, who is also a keen yachtsman and a yachtmaster, for reading my proofs and for some valuable comments and additions which have been included. Also the masters of the *Condor* vessels, who travel through the Channel Islands area each day, for their support.

Navigation and pilotage

Nautical miles, cables and metres

As the metric system is rapidly replacing imperial measures and since vertical heights and soundings are already shown in metres on charts, the practice in this edition will be to give short distances that the navigator is expected to estimate by eye in metres (m).

For these *estimated* distances, the navigator who normally estimates in cables and yards, can, to within 10%, take 200m as 1 cable (in fact 218·7yds) and 30m as 30yds (in fact 32·8yds).

However, since it is normal practice to use the latitude scale on a Mercator chart to measure nautical miles and tenths and, although the traditional cable is very close to a tenth of a nautical mile, when referring to a chart and especially when the required track may be plotted on the chart, distances will in most cases be given in nautical miles (M) and decimals (e.g. 3·8M, 0·3M).

Marks

Almost all Channel Islands pilotage depends on marks, since plotting a position on a chart from a fix will take too long. To qualify as a professional local pilot it is necessary to memorise the marks and transits as well as the tidal conditions and the names and drying heights of the more dangerous rocks in the area.

Note that positions are given in the text to the nearest tenth of a minute of latitude and longitude. A large-scale chart should be consulted for a more precise position.

Preparation

It is the intention that, when planning a visit to a particular area, this book should be consulted together with tide tables and charts of a suitable scale. Before setting out it will be essential to obtain a local weather forecast.

The transits for a particular passage are numbered and shown on one of the plans in the book, together with the true courses.

The plans *must on no account be used* for navigation or pilotage so it is advisable to plot the track on the chart in use, together with the courses or transit bearings (converted to magnetic).

It should be appreciated that light and weather conditions may not be the same as those when the transit photographs were taken. Binoculars are useful, and in many cases the shape of the skyline and other features shown in the photograph can help in identifying marks on shore, while the tide level must be taken into account when identifying beacons on rocks.

Some years ago an owner said to me: 'Transits and breast marks are not much use when I am doing fourteen knots in my motorboat.' Recently a French passenger boat struck a rock when travelling, I gather, at thirty knots through a narrow passage, requiring a sharp turn, using a rear transit.

Do not enter a passage until you are sure that the initial marks have been positively identified. Then proceed down the channel, with a hand-held compass, at such a speed that you are always sure of your position, have ample time to sight the next marks and, checking the bearings, to be well prepared for the alteration of course. Strong cross tides present a problem but, as long as the boat's speed is sufficient, a contrary stream in a channel can act as a useful brake. Travelling in the same direction as a strong stream in an unfamiliar, narrow channel is stressful and to be avoided.

GPS and radar

As an aid to the navigator and for safety purposes, it is advisable for a yacht to be equipped with GPS and, if possible, radar.

GPS and chart datum

At present the British Admiralty charts for the Channel Islands are prepared using European Datum while GPS operates on WGS 84. Before fixing a position with GPS, the chart datum should first be read and the necessary correction made.

The 'selective availability' errors introduced by the US Defense Department make it inadvisable to use GPS for pilotage among rocks.

Radar and the echosounder

Under most conditions at sea radar is a valuable aid for detecting above-water objects and an echosounder for determining the depth of a gradually shelving bottom.

It would be foolish to rely completely on either instrument for pilotage among rocks.

'Eyeball navigation'

For cautious inshore pilotage, a reliable chart, good visibility, binoculars, a hand-held compass and good eyesight are essential.

Level of difficulty of a passage

As with all pilotage, the passages described in this book must be taken at the owner's risk and careful preparation should be made before entry. It is the editor's opinion that they can be divided into three classes:

(Grade M) – Moderate – where normal caution will suffice.

(Grade EC) – Extra Care – where extra concentration is necessary.

(Grade H) – Hazardous – where it would be foolish to attempt the passage without a local expert on board.

In the text, the letters **(M)**, **(EC)** or **(H)** will be placed at the start of the directions for a passage or a part of a passage.

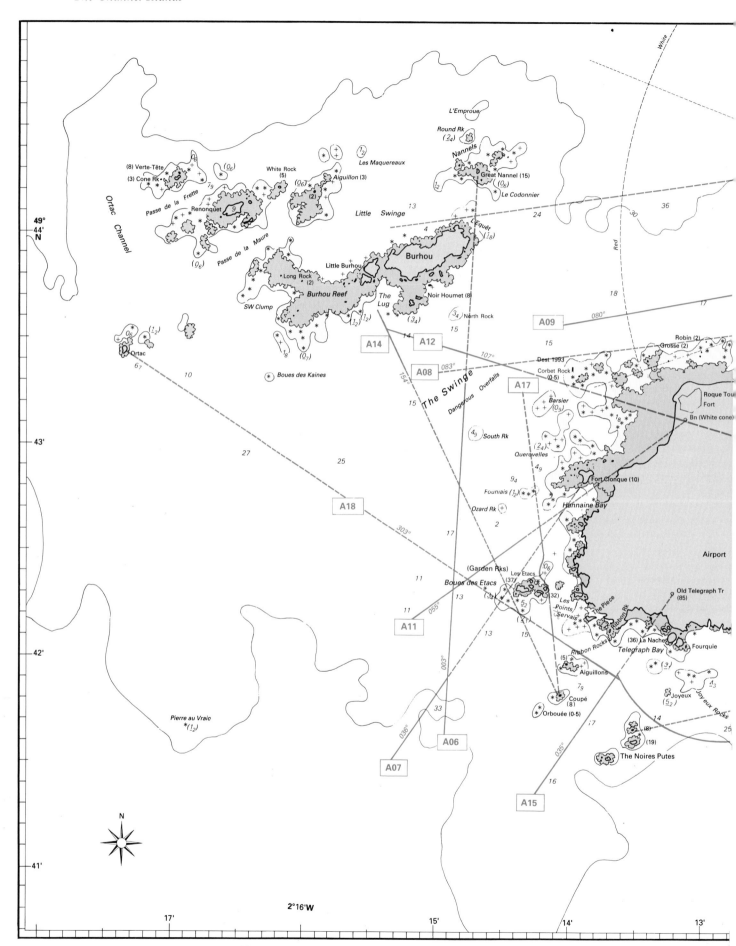

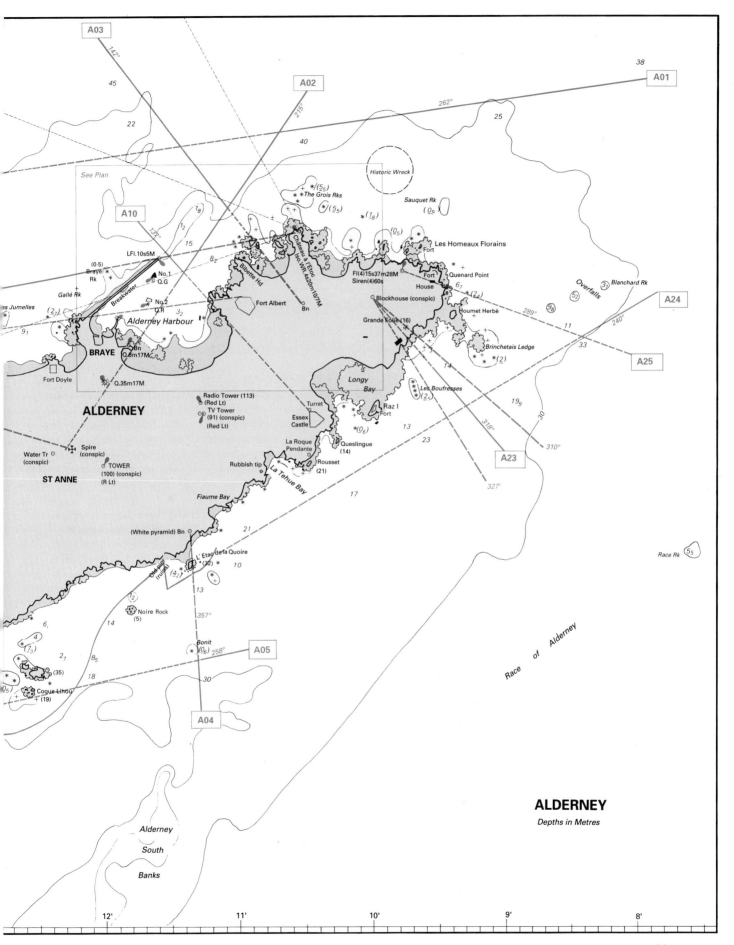

A03

142°

45

22

A02

215°

262°

38

A01

40

25

See Plan

Historic Wreck

Sauquet Rk

A10

131°

1₈

*(5₅)

* *The Grois Rks

(0₉)

1₂

(5₅)

15

*(1₈)

Les Homeaux Florains

LFI.10s5M

Château à l'Etoc

Iso.WR.4s20m10/7M

(0₅)

Fort

8₂

(0·5)

Braye
Rk

No.1
Q.G

Bibette Hd

Fl(4)15s37m28M

Siren(4)60s

Fort

Quenard Point

Blanchard Rk

Galle Rk

Breakwater

3₂

Fort Albert

Bn

House

Fort

6₇

*(2₄)

Overfalls

5₂

s Jumelles

(2₇)

No.2
Q.R

Blockhouse (conspic)

Houmet Herbé

9₈

A24

9₁

Alderney Harbour

Grande Folie (16)

Brinchetais Ledge

11

240°

289°

BRAYE

Bn
Q.8m17M

*(2)

33

A25

Fort Doyle

Q.35m17M

Longy
Bay

3

14

A23

310°

318°

319°

*** Les Boufresses

(2₅)

30

ALDERNEY

Radio Tower (113)
(Red Lt)

Turret

Raz I
Fort

19₉

TV Tower
(91) (conspic)
(Red Lt)

Essex
Castle

13

23

327°

Water Tr
(conspic)

Spire
(conspic)

La Roque
Pendante

Queslingue
(14)

*(0₆)

ST ANNE

TOWER
(100) (conspic)
(R Lt)

Rubbish tip

Rousset
(21)

La Tehue Bay

Fiaume Bay

17

(White pyramid) Bn

21

L'Etac de la Quoire
*(32) *

10

Old pier
(ruins)

(4₂)

13

Noire Rock
(5)

357°

6,

14

Bonit
*(0₆)

258°

A05

4

2₇

8₅

(7₃)

18

-30'

(35)

Coque Lihou
(19)

0₅

A04

Race Rk

5₅

Race   of   Alderney

ALDERNEY

Depths in Metres

Alderney

South

Banks

12'

11'

10'

9'

8'

Alderney

Quenard Point lighthouse 49°43'·8N 2°09ⁱ·8W

Vecta Riduna to the Romans, possibly derived from Ariduna to the Celts, the Alderney folk are called Ridunians. As with the other islands, the local patois is derived from Norman (Nordic) French and the written names of many of the rocks have a French look about them but when spoken they are hard to recognise:

Saye Bay – Soy Bay, Quoiré – Quire, Coupé – Coupe, Grois rocks – Groys, Noires Putes – Nurpitz, Corbet – Kerby, and Brinchetais – Brimtides!

The name Alderney (Aurigny in modern French) is derived from the Scandinavian *Aurin-ey*, a gravel or mudflat island.

Braye's sunken breakwater

In 1847 the construction of the breakwater and other naval works at Cherbourg caused concern to the British government. Forts were constructed in the Solent and on the Portsdown Hills to protect Portsmouth from a possible French invasion. Forts and Martello towers were built on the Channel Islands, and St Catherine's breakwater, Jersey and the breakwater at Braye were designed to shelter the British fleet.

After St Catherine's breakwater was built it was found that the water that it protected was too shallow for warships.

The breakwater at Braye was completed to a length of 4,800ft in 1864, working in depths of up to 20 fathoms and costing more than 1½ million pounds in those days. However, the planned construction for the rest of the harbour was not commenced. In 1872 the outer 1,900ft was abandoned and allowed to collapse, leaving the existing structure of 900m and a dangerous submerged reef of 600m, with a minimum depth of 1·2m at chart datum.

Exposed to Atlantic storms since then repairs to the existing wall have been costly.

Charts

Admiralty *2656, 2669, 3653, 60* and *SC60, 2845*
Imray *C33A*

Admiralty charts are based on European Datum. Positions obtained using WGS datum should be moved 0·06' northward and 0·09' eastward.

Lights

1. **Casquets** 49°43'·4N 2°22'·7W Fl(5)30s37m 24M Racon White tower, highest and NW of three
2. **Quenard Point lighthouse** 49°43'·8N 2°09'·8W Fl(4)15s37m28M Siren(4)60s 085°-vis-027° White tower, black band
3. **Château à l'Etoc** 49°44'·0N 2°10'·6W Iso.WR.4s20m10/7M 071°-R-111°-W-151° White column

4. **Alderney Harbour breakwater head** 49°43'·9N 2°11'·6W LFl.10s7m5M
5. **Braye Harbour Ldg Lts 215°**
   Front 49°43'·4N 2°11'·8W Q.8m17M 210°-vis-220° Synchronised with rear White column with yellow triangle on 2m concrete base, on elbow of Old Harbour Pier
   Rear 500m from front Q.35m17M 210°-vis-220° White column, with yellow rectangle, on 2m concrete base
6. **Braye Jetty head** 49°43'·6N 2°11'·9W 2F.R(vert)8m5M
7. **Buoys** Two starboard and two port buoys marking the fairway in the harbour. No. 1 starboard Q.G. No. 2 port Q.R. Second starboard Q(2)G.5s. Second port Q(2)R.5s.

Tidal levels referred to chart datum

Braye 49°43'·6N 2°11'·7W MHWS 6·3m MHWN 4·7m MLWN 2·6m MLWS 0·8m MTL 3·6m

Time differences for Braye on St Helier

St Helier	HW neaps	springs	LW neaps	springs
Braye	+0050	+0040	+0025	+0105

Tidal streams

The tidal streams and eddies round Alderney must be used to advantage. They cannot be fought! As with the Alderney Race, the Swinge should be avoided in bad weather conditions when the overfalls, seen from the safety of dry land, can be spectacular.

Overfalls

Reference to Admiralty *60* will show the positions of the overfalls surrounding the island. In calm weather, these can be avoided if necessary by inspection. In conditions of wind against tide however, they must be given a wide berth! According to locals, besides the Swinge, the area east of Quenard Point, surrounding Blanchard Rock and the Inner and Outer Race Rocks is best avoided. Even in slight conditions overfalls build and can be thought inspiring at low water with a strong south westerly.

The strength of the stream in the Swinge is greater on the Burhou side, particularly during the ebb. Due to the saddle between Corbet rock and Burhou the overfalls on the ebb (southwesterly flow) will be found in the southwest end of the Swinge, and during the flood (northeasterly flow) they build up further north, to the east of Burhou and Great Nannel.

The tidal stream diagrams on page 126-9, produced with the assistance of Brian Markell, show the flow round the island and a more general picture is obtained by reference to *NP 264 Admiralty Tidal Stream Atlas – Channel Islands*.

Two main points of interest are:
1. The almost continual set to the northeast, inshore along the southeast coast of Alderney, except between HW Braye +2½ and +4½ when it is not detectable.

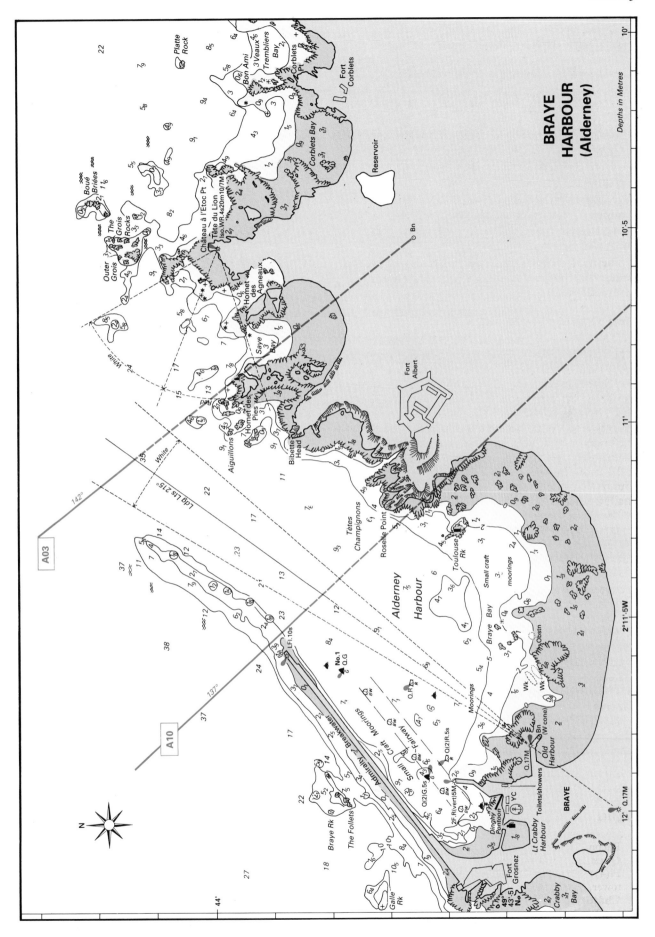

**BRAYE
HARBOUR
(Alderney)**

Depths in Metres

2. Three hours before local high water a vortex forms at the root and 2 hours before HW a northwest set commences over the sunken breakwater, reaching a maximum at HW. This turns to move southwest in a stream 100m wide along the full length of the breakwater and continues until slack water 2½ hours after local high. This stream can reach 4 knots at springs while, with a narrow band of dead water between, the northeasterly stream will also be running at 4 knots.

Approaches

The approaches to Alderney are simple, for the most part the island is steep-to and the only consideration is the strength of the tidal streams. The tidal range is half that of Jersey but, being west of the tip of the Cherbourg Peninsula, the streams are three times as strong. The effect produced by a SW breeze meeting a 7 knot ebb in the Swinge is spectacular and it is essential to time an arrival or departure at slack tide or with the assistance of wind with tide.

The main approaches are aimed at Braye Harbour which is the port of entry for visitors.

BRAYE FROM THE EAST OR NORTH

Clearing mark A01 262° – Casquets LtHo open to the north of Burhou Island, will clear the Grois Rocks to the north of the island. The Casquets are frequently lost in the haze. If so it is only necessary to keep ½M offshore until the entrance to the harbour opens. Then steer down on 215°, midway between the breakwater and the islets to the east with either:

Clearing mark A01

W Beacon

Transit A02 215° – The white pyramid on Douglas Quay midway between the church spire and the water tower.

or:

With the recently adjusted leading lights with a yellow triangle and rectangle on the columns in line on 215°. The lights are lit by day and, being bright, should be easy to pick up in haze or mist.

By night the leading lights on 215° will lead into the harbour. The white sector of the light on Château à l'Etoc (Iso.WR.4s) clears the end of the sunken breakwater when approaching from the north or northwest.

Braye Harbour from NE *Photo* Alderney Tourist Office/Brian Green

BRAYE FROM THE NORTHWEST

From the northwest by day, approach with Quenard Pt LtHo bearing no less than 120° and identify the leading beacons:

Transit A03 142° – beacons in line.

Hold this transit to clear the outer end of the submerged breakwater and, when the harbour opens, turn onto Transit A02 to enter.

Coming from the east, if from bad timing or under sail with a dying wind you find that the ebb is carrying you SW down the Race, do not fight it but make an approach from the south later.

The only isolated danger is Bonit (drying 0·6m) ½M offshore. The harbourmaster Steve Shaw took the editor over it and the striking marks are shown below. The rock is longer than the symbol on Admiralty *60* suggests and a yacht under sail in the tide should keep well clear.

By night, keep in the visible sector of Quenard LtHo (Fl(4)15s).

Bonit striking mark A04 357° – White pyramid to the right of l'Etac de la Quoiré.

Bonit striking mark A05 258° – The inner Noire Pute x the outer Coque Lihou.

BRAYE FROM THE SOUTH

With a fair tide the approach is through the Swinge (the name is a corruption of Passe au Singe, Monkey Passage).

Enter on a northerly course as Pierre au Vraic (drying 1·2m) lies 2M SW of Alderney. A safe transit is:

Transit A06 003° – Great Nannel open to the right of Burhou Island. This course leads well into the Swinge but, with Fort Clonque abeam to starboard, it will be necessary to come round on to 030° if the overfalls have built up east of Burhou Island.

At the top of the flood a better mark is:

Transit A07 036° – Fort Clonque open to the left of Les Etacs or 'Garden Rocks' with their vast colony of gannets (seen at LW).

When ½M off the Garden Rocks steer north into the Swinge.

A glance at the chart will show the extent of the off-lying reefs between the Garden Rocks and Alderney Harbour breakwater, the outermost drying rocks, from south to north, being: Founiais (drying 1·2m), Querouelles (drying 2·4m), Barsier (drying 0·9m) and Corbet Rock (0·5m above water) with a yellow beacon and radar reflector on a drying rock 200m to the NE. This beacon was destroyed in 1994 but should have been replaced by 1997.

Keep 0·75M offshore until:

Transit A08 083° – Left-hand end of Fort Albert over the left-hand end of the fort at the root of the breakwater.

This transit indicates that you are clear to the north of Corbet but do not steer in on 083° or you will be too close to the rocks, some of which are visible in the lower photo.

Continue north until:

Transit A09 080° – North side of Château à l'Etoc x north end of breakwater.

Follow this transit up to the breakwater head. The sunken breakwater presents a hazard but there is a relatively flat area, with a minimum depth of 2·3 m, 50m off the breakwater head. Not less than two hours either side of low water, when there is no ground sea running, the harbour may be entered with caution, using:

Transit A10 137° – 'Turret' on Fort Essex over gap in slope below Fort Albert. A bush has recently grown beside the turret (or 'Pepper Pot') as shown by the inset photo.

On approaching the Swinge, should the SW stream be running strongly, there are two anchorages where one can wait out of the tide.

HANNAINE BAY SOUTH OF FORT CLONQUE

The passage between rocks on either side is 200m wide and the transit should be held accurately:

Transit A11 055° – White pyramid beacon south of Roque Tourgis Fort midway between Fort Clonque and shore.

Anchor in 3m (sand) 100m or more south of Fort Clonque.

THE LUG OF BURHOU

In light winds from the south, this is a protected anchorage except at high water near springs when the stream rushes between Burhou and Little Burhou. It can be approached from the SW avoiding the overfalls in the Swinge if they are active.

A drying reef extends south and then west from Burhou with isolated rocks off the tip east of the entrance (see plan page 10–11).

To avoid these rocks, approaching from the south or east, use:

Transit A12 107° – White pyramid beacon south of Roque Tourgis Fort x church spire.

Hold this stern transit until the eastern edge of Little Burhou bears due north, then steer due north into the anchorage.

Anchor in 9m (sand) or, on soundings, closer to the drying rocks SW of Burhou.

Transit A14 154° – An alternative stern transit for entry or departure is with Coupé rock open to the west of the Garden Rocks on 154°.

It must be appreciated that a yacht leaving the Lug for Braye will have no option but to cross the overfalls area.

Braye Harbour

Braye Harbour Office VHF Ch 74, listen on 16 and 12.

Unless coming from Guernsey, a customs declaration must be made.

Facilities

In 1996 there were 80 visitors' moorings, two rows running parallel to the breakwater and 11 in Toulouse Bay. When anchoring, beware of the many isolated rocky patches in the bay.

Mainbrayce Chandlers and Engineers, in the inner harbour, provide fuel and a water taxi, VHF Ch 37 or 80.

Showers, toilets and telephones near the quay.

The yacht club welcomes visitors.

Supermarket, restaurants, a café, bars and bicycle hire nearby.

Three quarters of a mile up the hill, in the town of St Anne is a post office and a selection of banks, shops, restaurants and bars.

There are many pleasant walks and rides round the island.

Round the island

There are several anchorages that may be visited with an engine capable of at least 5 knots, in good, settled weather. The passage westabout round the island, including short visits to the bays, starting at half tide down (St Helier) should take about 9 hours, returning to Braye just before high water.

For a quick trip, without visits, leave Braye one hour before low water and, travelling at a minimum speed of 5 knots, arriving at the NE end of the island at slack water, return to Braye about four hours later. The local yacht race round the island has been completed in two hours!

Round the breakwater and take A10 as a stern transit, followed by A09 as a stern transit to enter the Swinge.

Once in the Swinge two passages are available, either outside the Garden Rocks (Les Etacs) or inside them. Hannaine Bay and Telegraph Bay may be visited.

OUTSIDE THE GARDEN ROCKS (Grade M)

Continue on A09 as a stern transit until Great Nannel bears due north, well open of Burhou. Then come round to the south and, with due allowance for the stream, get onto Transit A06 to leave the Garden Rocks 0·3M to port.

Before the Garden Rocks are abeam, Hannaine Bay may be entered and left using Transit A11 as on page 18.

With the Garden Rocks abeam, steer 160° to leave Orbouée (height 0·5m) 0·2M to port, with Coupé (8m high and looking like a volcano) inshore of Orbouée.

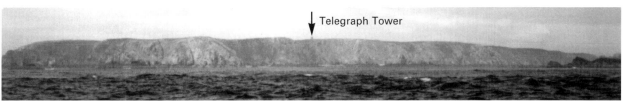

Telegraph Tower

Photo A15

See Photo A15. To enter Telegraph Bay, steer in on 035° midway between Coupé and the Noires Putes (Ner Puts) (height 19m, 14m and 8m). From well offshore the old telegraph tower (height 85m) makes a good mark.

See Photo A16. Telegraph Bay is a popular anchorage, with a long winding path up the cliff. It is however encumbered with rocks and Admiralty *60* should be consulted before entering.

Telegraph Tower

Photo A16

INSIDE THE GARDEN ROCKS
(Grade EC or perhaps H)

Mr Brian Markell has advised on this passage which he uses when taking visitors round the island, giving them a close view of the Gannet colony. Looking at Admiralty *60*, he informs me that the 0·6m patch with the + rock just south of it, 200m north of the most easterly, inner Garden Rock, are correctly placed, but the * rock by the 4·3m sounding is on a line between the north sides of the northernmost and easternmost of the Garden Rocks. This leaves a clear passage 20m off the two rocks.

The passage should be taken at low water when the heads in the centre of the gap, and one close to the inner Garden Rock, are exposed.

Brian avoids the strong flood stream in the Swinge by steering on Transit A17 when clear of Corbet Rock and passing inshore of Founiais.

The part of the transit A17 north of the A11 transit line *must not be used at low water springs* unless a local expert is on board as it is shallow and encumbered with rocks.

An alternative, when steering south with A06 as a stern transit, is to turn to port and take Transit A11 towards Hannaine Bay until Coupé appears just open of the inner Garden Rock.

Coupé

Transit A17 173° – Coupé open to the left of the inner Garden Rock.

Steer on this transit and, when 400m from the gap, steer for the northernmost Garden Rock until within 20–30m of it. This position is sheltered from the flood stream and affords a good view of the gannets.

Then steer to round the inner Garden Rock (height 32m) passing through the gap 20m from the head close to it, showing in the photo below Coupé.

Once through, steer for Coupé on 173° and look for Ortac (height 22m), with its white coating of bird lime, opening to the south of the Garden Rocks.

Photo for Transit A18 taken from the 035° approach line to Telegraph Bay.

Transit A18 303° When Ortac is bearing 303°, just to the left (south) of the rock arrowed

Ortac

Telegraph Bay at LW with Telegraph Tower over Joyeux Rk (dries 5.2m)

in A18, turn to port on 123° with this as a stern transit, keeping 250m off 'The Piece' to clear the reef and off Les Puits Jervais or 'Ribbon Rocks' (see plan page 10−11). Round into Telegraph Bay, when Coupé and Orbouée are in transit on 233°

Note that the line of rocks named Les Puits Jervais on Admiralty *60* are known locally as the Ribbon Rocks, and 'The Piece' is as shown on the plan.

If Ortac is lost in haze, on passing out through the gap continue to steer for Coupé and, when 300m from Aiguillons (height 5m) steer 220° to leave Orboué 300m to port and come round to enter Telegraph Bay with the telegraph tower on 035°.

LEAVING TELEGRAPH BAY AND CONTINUING EASTWARDS

With the rocks off La Nache and Joyeux (drying 5·2m) at the end of a reef west of Coque Lihou, a visitor should not pass inshore of Coque Lihou.

Steer out on 215° until Ortac is open south of the Garden Rocks (Transit A18 303°) or, if Ortac is invisible, the southern edge of the Garden Rocks on 310°. Then steer out on 130°, with due regard to the stream, leaving Joyeux to port and the Noires Putes to starboard and, when the tallest of the Noires Putes (19m) is abeam, turn east and, leaving Coque Lihou 200m to port, steer in to pass either side of Noire Roque (5m) but well inside Bonit (drying 0·6m).

Ruined pier   Noire Roque   La Roque Pendante   L'Etac de la Quoire

Photo A19

Noire Roque is an isolated rock (see Photo 19) and can be passed on either side giving it a wide berth to the NW and N, particularly at low water as reefs run off the main rock. Passing inshore, one can visit the ruined pier, Cachalière, once used for loading granite. On inspection of Admiralty *60* it can be seen that east of the pier, l'Etac de la Quoiré (32m) has heads and above-water rocks to the SW and NE so: leave the pier steering south until clear, when it is possible to steer 060° 80m off la Quoiré with its above-water rocks, turn to port when the northeastern rock is abeam to pass inshore of the three drying rocks 250m E and SE of la Quoiré, for a visit to Fiaume Bay.

FIAUME BAY (LES BECQUET) (See Photo A20)

To enter this attractive bay, Admiralty *60* shows the drying rock off the southern point and, approaching from the SW, the clearing mark for this rock is with the whole of the ruined pier visible between l'Etac and cliff. When the centre of the bay bears 305° turn on this course and anchor on soundings.

Photo A20

LA TCHUE BAY (see Photo A21)

This bay affords the next but rather less attractive anchorage, with the burning rubbish tip on the cliffs above. It may be entered with reference to Admiralty *60* and the spectacular La Rocque Pendante may be seen hanging out of the cliff to the east.

Photo A21

LONGY BAY

This bay can be used with care when awaiting the tide. Admiralty *60* shows the dangers west of Raz Island and it is best to enter leaving Queslingue (height 14m) 100m to port and the rock drying 0·6m to starboard.

Breast mark A22

Breast mark A22 223°. Anchor when La Rocque Pendant is over the end of the curved end of the wall. The photo shows a private mooring and the anchorage is nearer to the wall.

BAIE DU GOURNARD

The last bay, used to await the tide before rounding the NE end of the island is the Baie du Gournard. This is south of the fort on Houmet Herbé and protected to some extent by the Brinchetais or 'Brimtides' Ledge although the SW-going stream can run through the gap at 10 knots!

The Lug of Burhou anchorage at LW. Garden Rocks rear left

Passage inside the Garden Rocks at LW looking north

The Garden Rocks at half-tide. Fort Clonque over left-hand rock.
Photo Peter Carnegie

Coming from the SW, the clearing mark for Les Boufresses is with *Rousset well open to the east of Queslingue on 242°*.

Enter with due regard to the stream on:

Transit A23 318° – German blockhouse midway between the Grande Folie (height 16m) and the white house.

Anchor on sand in 3m outside the rocks shown on Admiralty 60.

The Baie du Gournard is a good anchorage except when winds are from the SW through to SE and is used by French yachts.

When leaving Baie du Gournard, steer southeast until the Brinchetais Ledge may be cleared. The clearing marks are:

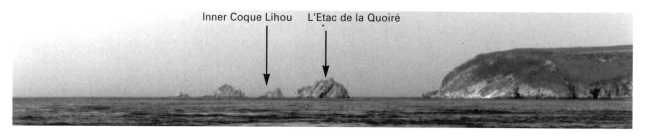

Clearing marks A24 240° – The innermost Coque Lihou open east of la Quoiré.

Steer NE with Coque Lihou well open of la Quoiré until:

Clearing marks A25 289° – Quenard LtHo is over a small grey house with black roof and a chimney at each end.

Then steer north taking care to avoid the overfalls round Blanchard Rock

Local boats use an inshore passage round the NE end of the island and may visit the two anchorages west of the lighthouse, shown on Admiralty 60. These anchorages are unsafe and visitors are advised to proceed round north of Sauquet Rock (drying 0·9m).

Photo A26

Quenard lighthouse with Braye Harbour in the background

This rock presents a hazard and, in order to clear it, make sure that the whole of the light tower (white/black/white) is visible above the fort Homeaux Florains. See photo A26.

Steering north,with due regard to the Blanchard Rock overfalls, when Quenard lighthouse is abeam to port come round to the northwest and, leaving Sauquet Rk to port, regain Transit A01 to approach the entrance to Braye Harbour.

Guernsey

Situated as it is, further from France, Guernsey is less commercialised than Jersey but is fortunate to possess two excellent harbours, built in the nineteenth century, when granite and shipbuilding were important to the island. St Peter Port handles passengers and containers while St Sampson deals with oil, coal, timber and stone.

The economy of the island relies heavily on the tourist, and visitors in boats are welcomed and well provided for, with three marinas and all the facilities that go with them. St Peter Port is a popular stopping off point for yachts cruising to North Brittany. Fuel in the Channel Islands is duty free while diesel in France is expensive.

Besides several pretty anchorages to be explored by boat, hire cars, scooters and an excellent bus service make an exploration of inland Guernsey well worthwhile.

Charts

Admiralty *2669, 3654, 807, 808.* Photocopies of the older charts *3400* and *262 a, b* and *c* may be obtainable from the Hydrographic Office. The new Admiralty charts are based on European Datum. Imray *C33A*

Lights for approaches to St Peter Port

1. **Les Hanois** 49°26'·2N 2°42'·1W Fl(2)13s33m20M Horn(2)60s 294°-vis-237° Grey stone tower, black lantern. Helicopter platform. 1·27M ESE, on Pleinmont Point single mast 2F.R lights, 1m apart. Single F.R light on German watch tower 400m NxW of mast.

Little Russel

2. **Platte Fougère** 49°30'·9N 02°29'W Fl.WR.10s15m16M Horn 45s 155°-W-085°-R-155° White octagonal tower, black band Racon 'P'
3. **Tautenay** 49°30'·2N 2°26'·7W Q(3)WR.6s7m7/6M 050°-W-215°-R-050° Black and white beacon
4. **Petite Canupe** 49°30'·2N 2°29'·1W Q(6)+LFl.15s ↯ card beacon
5. **Roustel** 49°29'·3N 2°28'·9W Q.10m7M Lattice structure
6. **Platte** 49°29'·1N 2°29'·5W Fl.WR.3s6m7/5M 024°-R-219°-W-024° Green conical tower
7. **Brehon** 49°28'·3N 2°29'·2W Iso.4s19m9M Beacon on round tower
8. **St Martin's Point** 49°25'·37N 2°31'·61W Fl(3)WR.10s15m14M. Horn(3)30s. White building flat roof. 185-R-191°-W-011°-R-081°

Lit buoys

9. **Reffée** 49°27'·8N 2°31'·81W ↯ card VQ(6)+LFl.10s
10. **Lower Heads**. 49°29'·91N 2°28'·48W ↯ card Q(6)+LFl.15s Bell

Big Russel

11. **Noire Pute** 49°28'·3N 2°24'·9W Fl(2)WR.15s8m6M 220°-W-040°-R-220° On rock
12. **Fourquies** 49°27'·40N 2°26'·40W Q ↟ card buoy

Beaucette Marina

14. **Ldg Lts** 276°49°30'·25N 2°30'·13W
    Front F.R *Rear* 185m from front F.R

4. **Petite Canupe** ↯ card beacon (see above), left to starboard on approach.

St Sampson

15. **Ldg Lts 286°** 49°29'N 2°31'W
    Front S pier hd F.R.3m5M 230°-vis-340°
    Rear 390m from front on clock tower F.G.13m
16. **N Pier Hd** 49°29'N 2°30'·7W F.G.3m5M 230°-vis-340° Post
17. **Crocq Pier** 49°29'N 2°31'·1W F.R.11m5M 250°-vis-340° Red column Traffic signals.

Queen Elizabeth II Marina

18. 49°27'·79N2°31'·78W DirOc.WRG.3s5m6M 258°-G-268°-W-272°-R-282°
9. **Reffée** s card buoy (see above), left to starboard on approach

St Peter Port

19. **Castle breakwater head Ldg Lts 220°** 49°27'·4N 2°31'·4W
    Front Al.WR.10s14m16M Horn 15s 187°-vis-007° Synchronised with horn Dark tower, white on NE side RC
    Rear Belvedere Oc.10s61m14M 179°-vis-269° White square, orange stripe, on white tower 217°-intens-223°
20. **White Rock pierhead** 49°27'·4N 2°31'·5W Oc.G.5s11m14M 174°-intens-354° Stone tower white lantern Traffic signals
21. **Victoria Marina Ldg Lts 265°** 49°27'·4N 2°31'·9W
    Front on S pier hd Oc.R.5s10m14M White framework tower, red top
    Rear 160m from front Iso.R.2s22m3M 260°-vis-270°

Tidal levels referred to chart datum

St Peter Port 49°27'N 2°31'W MHWS 9·3m MHWN 7·0m MLWN 3·6m MLWS 1·5m MTL 5·3m

Tidal streams

Guernsey is stuck out in the main tidal stream as much as Alderney, but since the shape is different, offshore the streams aren't as swift. However at springs the stream runs up to six knots at St Martin's Point, Lower Head buoy, Big Russel, Roustel and Platte Boue. When the barometer is reading below 1012 millibars and the wind is between W and SW the north and east-going streams will run longer and stronger.

Up to 600m from the Castle breakwater light an inshore tide runs south at half tide down and north at half tide up while there is slack water in the Russel.

The fact that the island enjoys hot weather during the summer months has an effect on the tide in the Russel. A set of up to 2 knots can be observed, running SE 0·4M to 0·5M NE of St Peter Port, 2 hours before high water when the current should be going the other way. (See Guernsey tidal charts page 130–132.)

Approaching Guernsey, St Peter Port

It is most likely that visitors will make St Peter Port their first port of call as there is still a requirement to clear customs on landing, although this may be done at Beaucette Marina.

Coming from Cherbourg or Alderney it is usual to approach St Peter Port through the Little Russel, although the Big Russel is a popular alternative. Yachts coming from the West Country can pass west of the Traffic Separation Scheme off the Casquets and, in good visibility, enter the Little Russel, leaving Platte Fougère lighthouse well to starboard.

Preferably, from the West Country, if a position west of Les Hanois lighthouse is reached 3½ hours before HW St Helier, the west-going Channel stream will have been setting the yacht clear of the Separation Scheme and a fair stream will take her along the south coast, to arrive at St Martin's point as the stream starts to run north into the Little Russel. Then, arriving at St Peter Port 2 hours before HW, it will be possible to pass over the sill into the visitors' yacht basin.

LITTLE RUSSEL

Approaching the channel from the Alderney Race, particularly in poor visibility, it is important, with a south-going stream, to pass to the west of the Banc de la Schôle as there is a southeasterly set and the first sighting of the Grande Amfroque (see picture page 55) could be to starboard with uncomfortable consequences.

NOTE

The senior St Peter Port pilot, Captain Morey warns that yachts under sail, coming from Cherbourg or Alderney will tend to arrive at LW when the SE stream through Le Boursée channel is strongest and can sweep a yacht onto the Humps.

He states that Transit G02 220° should only be used south of Roustel and that yachts under sail or without adequate power should approach by night with Roustel (Q) in line with Brehon (Iso.4s) 198° and turn onto G02 on approaching Roustel.

By day, when Roustel will be hard to identify from a distance, Transit G04 208° may be used initially and, with a careful check on the eastward set, when Tautenay is abeam, steer to starboard towards the Roustel x Brehon transit.

1. LITTLE RUSSEL FROM THE NORTH (2m) (WEST OF ROUSTEL)

By day

It is fortunate that St Peter Port, unlike St Helier, both faces east and is sheltered from the east by a group of islands (Herm, etc.).

Note that the old Roustel beacon tower was destroyed in 1993 and has been replaced by an unremarkable lattice structure. The black/white chequered base is covered at HW

Transit G02 220° – Belvedere rear leading Lt x Castle breakwater Lt (not in transit in photo).

Until Roustel is approached, this transit should really only be taken under power or at slack water (see note above). It passes only 0·5M NW of Platte Boue (drying 1·8m), but if you can see the mainland of Sark to the east of Grande Amfroque you are clear. A striking mark for this rock is: the two beacons on Grande Amfroque in line on 152°.

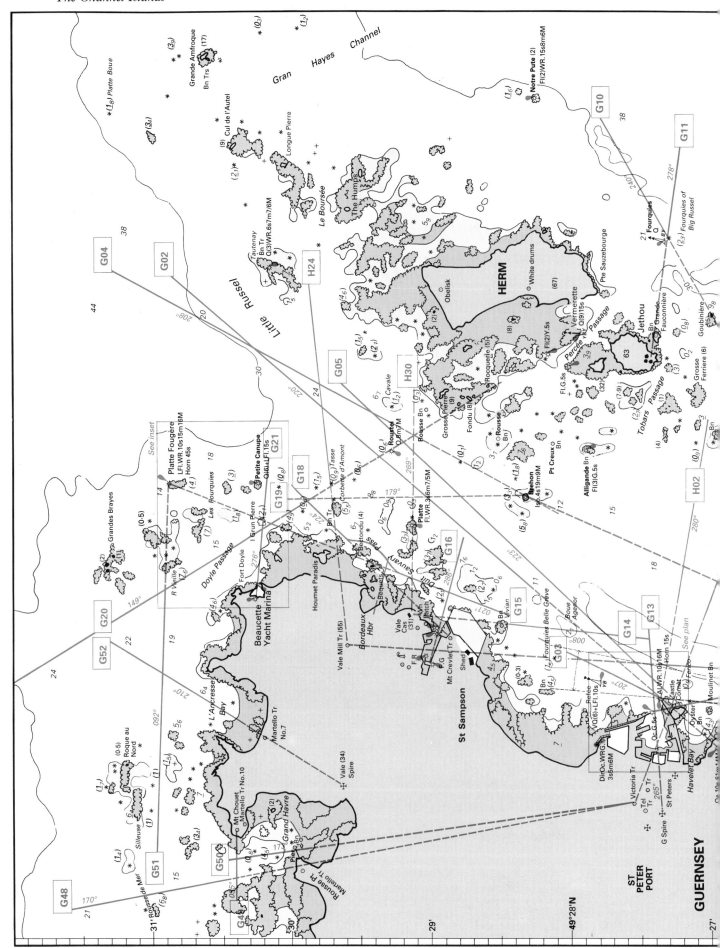

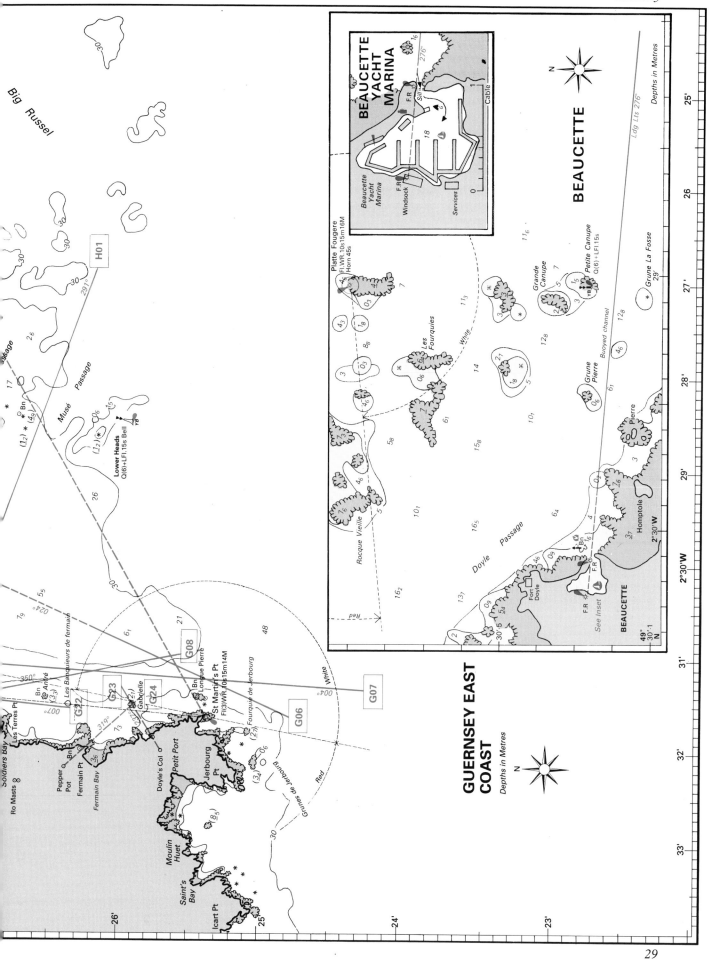

BEAUCETTE
YACHT
MARINA

Beaucette Yacht Marina

Windsock

F.R

Services

F.R

Sill

Cable

Depths in Metres

BEAUCETTE

Ldg Lts 276

Platte Fougere
Fl.WR.10s15m16M
Horn 45s

Les Fourquies

White

Grande Canupe

Petite Canupe
Q(6)+LFl.15s

Grune La Fosse

Grune Pierre

Buoyed channel

Pierre

Homptole

Rocque Vieille

Doyle   Passage

Fort Doyle

F.R

Bn

See Inset

BEAUCETTE

Red

H01

Big Russel

Musé   Passage

Passage

Lower Heads
Q(6)+LFl.15s Bell

Bn

Les Barduleurs de fermain

St Martin's Pt
Fl(3)WR.10s15m14M

Bn
Longue Pierre

Fourquie de Jerbourg

Gabrielle

Soldiers Bay

Les Terres Pt

Pepper Pot

Fermain Pt

Bn

Fermain Bay

Doyle's Col

Petit Port

Jerbourg Pt

Grunes de Jerbourg

Red

White

Moulin Huet

Saint's Bay

Icart Pt

GUERNSEY EAST COAST

Depths in Metres

N

G08

G23

G22

G24

G06

G07

Transit G03 207° – White patch on Castle Cornet open to the east (left) of Castle breakwater Lt clears all the drying dangers in Belle Grève Bay. Several yachts have hit the Fourquies of Belle Grève near LW!

By night
Transit G02 220° is used, the rear[19] light Oc.10s61m 14M and front[19] Al.WR.10s14m16M. This transit is easier to see by night than by day, but as it passes over Boue Agenor (depth 2·1m) which is guarded by the red sector of Platte[6] (Fl.WR.3s) it is necessary for deep-draught vessels to borrow 100m to port when abreast of Brehon Tower.

A useful alternative approach by day or night is to put Roustel[5] (Q.8m7M) on Brehon[7], 198°. Coming from the NW you are safe in the visible sector of Sark light (Fl.15s65m20M), on 138° or more.

2. LITTLE RUSSEL FROM THE NORTH (6m) (EAST OF ROUSTEL)
By day only
The transits are more easily seen from a distance than the previous marks.

Transit G04 208° – St Martin's Point just to the right of Brehon Tower.

See panoramic sketch G01 below.

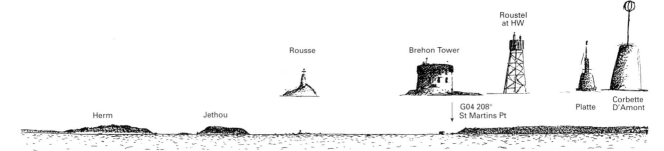

400m before coming to Roustel change to:

Transit G05 223° – Belvedere House x Castle Cornet white patch.

3. LITTLE RUSSEL FROM THE SOUTH
By day
No marks are needed and you can enter anywhere between Lower Heads buoy and a point 800m east of St Martin's Point.

Rounding St Martin's Point from the west keep at least ½M clear.

The Fourquie de Jerbourg and Grunes de Jerbourg provide work for the lifeboat every summer owing to the tidal set.

Do not turn north until:

Transit G06 024° – Brehon Tower bearing 024° and well open to east of Longue Pierre beacon (yellow with red 'L' and 'P').

Note that Brehon Tower in transit with Longue Pierre is a striking mark for the Fourquie.

Next take:

Transit G07 004° – Vale Mill over the right-hand green-roofed shed leads up the Little Russel. This book's transit replaces the one on Admiralty 807 and 808. It is a long transit and as an alternative:

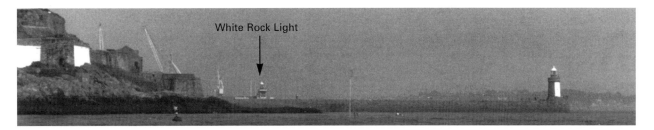

Clearing mark G08 350° – White Rock Lt (Oc.G.5s) open to the right of Castle Cornet clears dangers off the coast as far as Oyster beacon. More than 200m NE of Oyster lies Ferico rock (depth 0·8m) and before passing Oyster take:

Transit G09 304° – St Peter Port pierheads open.

By night

Making a landfall anywhere near St Martin's Point, make sure that you can see Les Hanois Lt[1] (Fl(2)13s33m20M). The obscured section covers most of the dangers on the south coast. The red sector of St Martin's[8] (Fl(3)WR.10s) is only to guard the rocks just off the point, so come to the east until White Rock light[20] is just visible to the east of Castle Point.

4. BIG RUSSEL FROM NORTHWARD

When beating down to St Peter Port by day from the northeast against a southwester, the Big Russel provides a channel seldom less than 2½M wide between Herm and Sark which is largely free of traffic.

Apart from overfalls there are only two offlying dangers: Noir Pute (2m) is marked by a lit beacon[11] (Fl(2)WR.15s) and Fourquies (drying 2·3m) marked by a lit N card buoy[12].

The striking marks for Fourquies are a guide when tacking as the buoy is frequently off station.If you can see Brehon Tower between Herm and Jethou you are clear to the NE.

Once round the Lower Heads buoy[10] (S card Q(6)+LFl.15s) you can head off for St Peter Port.

Striking mark G10 240° – St Martins Pt over Goubinière.

Striking mark G11 278° – A cluster of rocks on the south slope of Jethou over Grande Fauconnière Bn.

ENTRY TO ST PETER PORT

White Rock port control 49°27'·43N 2°31'·50W

VHF Ch 12, Victoria Marina Ch 20 and 80. Water taxi Ch 10.
Except when arriving from Alderney, a customs declaration must be made.
Photo G12 shows the marks on the skyline behind the harbour.

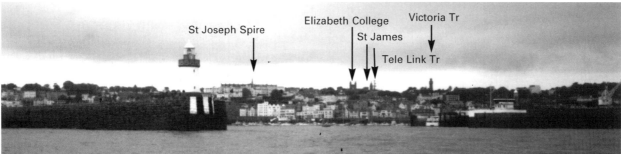

Photo G12

Boats of less than 15m LOA should enter under power, with due regard to traffic and keeping clear of the fairway if the port control is displaying a F.R light (entry prohibited for vessels over 15m).

Correction

In March 1997, at low water springs, while on the striking mark line G11, the Fourquies rock was observed to be about 400 metres north of this line. The rock was on the G10 line (240°) which is therefore correct as a striking mark. It was observed that the cluster of rocks on the south slope of Jethou would be obscured by Grande Fauconnière on the 278° transit and estimated that they would show as in the photo for G11 on a bearing of 284°. For safety, when approaching herm from the east, do not pass to the south of the Fourquies N card buoy and, when proceeding down the Big Russel, keep well to the east of the G10 transit until Goubinière is almost to starboard.

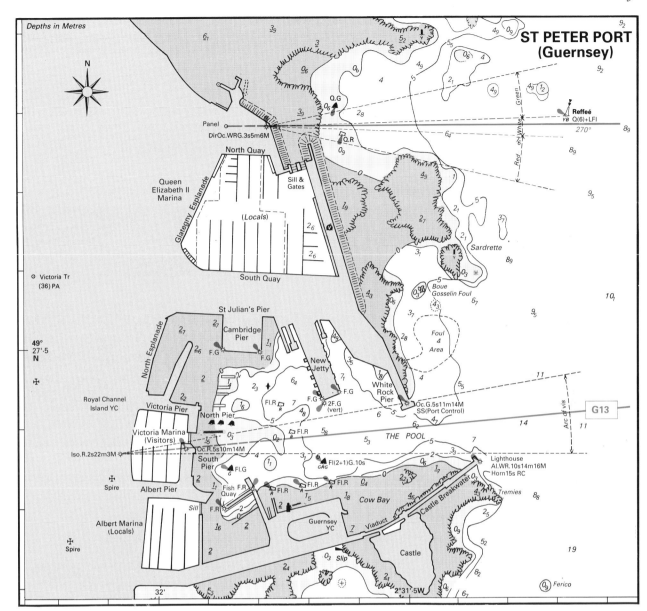

Depths in Metres

N

Victoria Tr (36) PA

49° 27'·5 N

Royal Channel Island YC

North Esplanade

Glategny Esplanade

Queen Elizabeth II Marina

North Quay

(Locals)

South Quay

Panel
DirOc.WRG.3s5m6M

Sill & Gates

Q.G

Q.R

Reffée
Q(6)+LFl
270°

Sardrette

Boue Gosselin Foul

Foul Area

St Julian's Pier

Cambridge Pier

F.G

F.G

New Jetty

Fl.R

F.G

2F.G (vert)

White Rock Pier

Oc.G.5s11m14M
SS(Port Control)

G13

Arc of vis

Victoria Pier

North Pier

Victoria Marina (Visitors)

Iso.R.2s22m3M

Oc.R.5s10m14M

South Pier

Fl.R

Fl.G

THE POOL

Fl(2+1)G.10s

Lighthouse
Al.WR.10s14m16M
Horn15s RC

Spire

Albert Pier

Albert Marina (Locals)

Sill

Fish Quay
F.R

F.R

Fl.R

Fl.R

Fl.R

Cow Bay

Castle Breakwater

Tremies

Guernsey YC

Viaduct

Castle

Spire

Slip

2°31'·5W

Ferico

32'

St Peter Port from the SE. *Photo* Patrick Roach

Looking S over the QE2 Marina at low water

St Sampson's commercial port. *Photo* Patrick Roach

G Spire

Leading Light tower

Transit G13 265° – Green church spire over Victoria Marina light tower may be used for entry by day and is lit for entry by night.

Front[21] (on light tower) Oc.R.5s10m14M. Rear[21] (on building behind) Iso.R.2s22m3M.

In the harbour, the channel to the Victoria Marina, waiting pontoon and berthing pontoons is on the south side, marked by lit buoys (see plan page 33).

The marina sill is 4·2m above chart datum and entry (controlled by red and green lights) is possible three hours either side of HW. Berths are allocated by marina staff in launches or a pontoon mooring may be taken in the harbour.

Facilities

All facilities are available in the port, with regular ferry services to the UK, France and to the other Channel Islands, and flights to the UK, Jersey, Alderney and Dinard.

The town is well supplied with post office, banks, shops, chandlers, engineers, restaurants, hotels and bars.

HAVELET BAY

Havelet Bay, south of Castle Cornet, provides a sheltered anchorage for those who do not wish to enter a crowded harbour. Visitors are still required to fill in a customs form on landing.

Enter between Oyster (yellow with red 'O' topmark) and Moulinet (yellow with red 'M' topmark) beacons and take a mooring, or anchor in 1–7m with due regard to some rocky patches on both sides of the bay.

A dinghy landing slip is situated just west of Castle Cornet and close to the yacht club building.

In summer, buoys are laid marking a passage into Havelet.

QUEEN ELIZABETH II MARINA (QE2)

This marina in the northern part of St Peter Port was constructed for local boat owners. It may be possible for visitors to obtain a berth for an extended stay on application to the local port authority on VHF Ch 12, or better, when in the harbour, by contact on Ch 80 with the dories from the Victoria Marina.

Entry is over a sill (drying 4·5m). A gate over the sill is lowered about 2½ hours either side of HW. A green light shows when there is 2m over the sill. Red light, no entry.

The approach is on a westerly transit of 270° passing close south of Reffée S card light buoy. The leading marks are two rather inconspicuous panels in line above a white patch on the loose rocks of the breakwater north of the entrance. The front panel is yellow with a RWG directional light and the rear panel is a red square attached to a lamp post. The channel is buoyed and, when 40m from the breakwater, turn hard to port round the inner port-hand buoy to enter the marina.

At night a directional light[18] Oc.WRG.3s (258°-G-268°-W-272°-282°) is used for the approach.

NORTH TO ST SAMPSON, BEAUCETTE MARINA AND THE DOYLE PASSAGE

Leaving St Peter Port take:

Transit G14 008° – Vivian pyramid with black/white bands, under the right-hand edge of Vale Castle. When 400m from Vivian turn to starboard to enter the Duit Sauvary Passage (the locals now call the passage 'the Birdo') and take:

Transit G15 021° – Platte Fougère light tower slightly left of centre between Bequets and Bectondu (height 4·4m). In the photo Houmet Paradis is showing behind Bequets.

ST SAMPSON SOUTH PIERHEAD

49°28'·97N 2°30'·66W VHF Ch 12

This transit leads past the commercial Port St Sampson, which dries and does not cater for visiting yachts. It may be entered on:

Transit G16 286° – The clock tower x white band on the southern breakwater head. The marks are lit for night entry (rear F.G and front F.R).

BORDEAUX HARBOUR

An inspection at HW of this drying harbour just north of St Sampson may be of interest if the yacht can take the ground.

Photo G17 provides a general view at half tide and the inset shows the leading mark for entry, a white post on the end of a pier, which covers at HW, in line with the end gable of a house (now obscured by trees!) on 290°. The rock Joumelle with its vertical end has a long flat spur (about to uncover in the inset photo) extending some 12m. The transit should be held until about 30m from Joumelle then turn to port and round the spur to enter the harbour.

Photo G17
Bordeaux Harbour

Continuing north after passing St Sampson and before Becquets is abeam to port, turn out to starboard and handrail round Bectondu, leaving it 150m to port, to take as:

Stern Transit G18 224° – Mont Crevlet Martello tower x *the more western of the two heads of Bectondu.*

The Duit Sauvary Passage will either lead into the Doyle Passage or clear out east of Platte Fougère to Alderney and the Race.

DOYLE PASSAGE

Leave the Duit Sauvary Passage when:

Stern Transit G19 179° – Brehon Tower its own width to the left of Corbette d'Amont and when:

Stern Transit G20 149° – Roustel midway between Herm and Jethou and in transit with the right-hand edge of Fondu, turn into the Doyle Passage on the reciprocal 329°.

The Doyle Passage leads out clear of Guernsey to the northwest, crossing the approach channel for Beaucette and the inshore passages along Guernsey's north coast.

BEAUCETTE MARINA 49°30'·14N 2°30'·10W

This marina, created by blasting a narrow gap in the rim of an old stone quarry more than 20m deep, may be approached from the Little Russel, south of Petite Canupe S card beacon[4] (Q(6)+ LFl.15s).

Transit G21 276° – Front, a red pole over the white patch on the north head. Rear, the wind-sock pole on the marina building.

For a night entry the leading marks are fitted with F.R lights[14].

The approach channel is marked by four red and four green buoys.

Since the Petite Canoupe beacon pole is hard to pick up and the leading marks are invisible from a distance, particularly in the evening sun, a RW fairway buoy should be in position at the entrance of the channel, south of Petite Canupe (1996).

The rocks on either side of the entrance are painted white, and 20m inside, piles of white painted motor tyres, ringing posts, provide a wave breaker.

The sill dries 2·4m and figures showing the depth over the sill are painted on the north head. Three or more waiting buoys are provided north of the entrance if there is insufficient depth for entry. Anchoring is not advised as the bottom is fouled by old chain and mooring blocks.

Beware of the drying rock 70m off the north head (this may be marked in 1997). When picking a mooring, turn out of the channel leaving the innermost green buoy close to port and, when entering the marina from the moorings, pass outside the green buoy, leaving it to starboard.

On entering, turn to port round the motor tyres and proceed to a pontoon berth in the deep water of a quarry. Priority is given to vessels leaving.

Facilities

VHF Ch 80. Customs forms are provided for visitors in the marina office.

Water and electricity on the pontoons. Slipway, 16-tonne travel-lift, showers and toilets, launderette, restaurant and shop. Diesel fuel, *Camping Gaz* and *Calor Gas*. Taxi service. Village stores are a short walk away as is a bus service to Town.

Beaucette Marina looking W. *Photo* Patrick Roach

St Peter Port to Rocquaine Bay, southabout

Chart

Admiralty *807*

Opinions vary and locals have their preferences for close inshore passages, and the editor is most grateful for the advice and assistance given by Captain Bob Morey (St Peter Port pilot), Captain Barry Paint (St Sampson pilot), and Messrs David Nicole and John Frankland.

Captain Paint, who trains pilots, comments that people will differ in their interpretation of a view and that lighting and the state of the tide can affect comparisons with the photos in the book.

The pilots use rocks as marks in many cases and visitors may not find identification easy when in a tight corner, with the tide running. Where possible, identifiable landmarks are used for the transits in this book and passages have been chosen accordingly.

A visit to Rocquaine Bay is best taken in calm, settled weather, with attention paid to local streams.

Should the intention be to circumnavigate the island, the trip should be taken in easy stages. However, to go right round in a day, the advice is to start from St Peter Port, with an engine capable of 5 or 6 knots, an hour after the morning HW springs, when for most of the day the south and west coasts should be swell free. Aim to arrive off Grande Havre near LW when the rocks will be exposed.

Reference to the tidal diagrams will show that the stream will assist as far as Rocquaine Bay and, up to LW St Peter Port, can provide a useful brake when identifying marks on the northwest coast. For identification, visibility should be at least 5M and preferably 7M.

Once familiar with the marks, a circumnavigation in one day is best made in an anticlockwise direction, starting from St Peter Port half an hour before half tide down when the tidal streams will be favourable all round the island.

SOUTHABOUT

Starting from Havelet Bay an inshore passage will first be described with some choice of alternative transits to Pleinmont Point clear of outlying dangers.

Passages used by locals inside Les Sept Boues and Les Kaines d'Amont, with the transit (Les Fontenelles partly hidden by trees) shown on Admiralty *807* and the anchorage east of Point de la Moye, are not included.

Entry to Rocquaine Bay should NOT be attempted unless the navigator is quite sure of the marks.

(Grade M)

Leaving Havelet Bay and rounding Moulinet beacon, take as a stern transit:

Transit G22 007° Oyster beacon open to the right of Castle breakwater light.

Soldiers Bay with a sandy beach, less popular than Fermain Bay, can be entered just south of Les Terres Point with its drying spur of rocks extending about 200m SE. Anchor on soundings as close as the tide allows.

Leave the bay on a course of 090° to clear a rock, Sablon (awash at LAT), and regain the stern transit G22.

This will take you inside Anfré beacon and Les Banquiers de Fermain (depth 0·9m) and outside Sablon and Goldfisher rock (drying 3·4m, not 2·1m as on Admiralty *807*) and the drying rocks off Fermain Point.

To avoid the reef off Fermain Point, enter Fermain Bay when you can see clear through the gap in the wall to the left of the Martello tower (see G24 below, where the gap is not fully open), and anchor on sand as close inshore as soundings and tide permit.

Leaving Fermain Bay on a reciprocal course, take as a stern transit G07 (page 31) or G08 (page 31) to pass outside Gabrielle Rock (drying 2·1m).

Scores of people have hit Gabrielle and two striking marks are provided to indicate its position.

Doyle's Column

Striking mark G23 237° – Doyle's Column conspicuous on the skyline above the trees, in line with white triangle with red border, less conspicuous on a post above the shoreline.

Pepper Pot

Lower mark

Striking mark G24 319° – White conical stone sentry box, 'The Pepper Pot', inconspicuous between trees on the skyline above Fermain Point, in line with a small white circular mark with red surround in the bushes below. Do not confuse this with a square white notice board for walkers, below and to the left of it.

Continue south, leaving Longue Pierre (yellow beacon with a red 'LP' topmark) more than 200m to starboard and countering any set onto the dangerous Fourquie de Jerbourg (drying 2·7m). Do not turn west until:

Transit G25

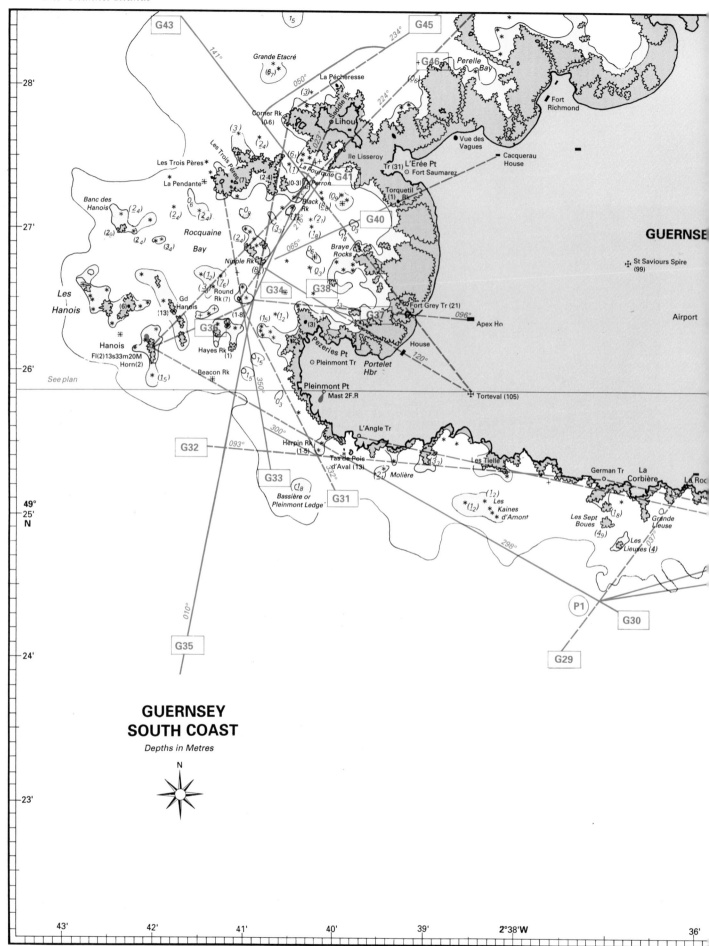

G43

G45

1₅

Grande Etacré
(6₇)

La Pécheresse

(3)

G46
Perelle Bay

Corner Rk
(0·6)

Saddle Rk

Fort
Richmond

Lihou

(3)
(2₄)

Les Trois Pères

(6₁)
(1)

Ile Lisseroy

L'Erée Pt

Vue des
Vagues

Cacquerau
House

Les Trois Pères (7)

La Rouquie
Perron

Tr (31)
Fort Saumarez

La Pendante

(2·4)
(0·3)

Banc des
Hanois

(2₄)

0·6

Black
Rk

0·9

Torquetil (1)
Bk

(2₄)
(2₄)

0·9

G41

(0·9)

GUERNSE

(2₀)

(2₄)
(3₄)

Rocquaine
Bay

(2₄)

(3·3)

(2₁)

G40

0·3

St Saviours Spire
(99)

(1·8)

Braye
Rocks

(0·8)

Nipple Rk

(8)

0·6

(0·3)

Les
Hanois

(1₂)
(1₆)

(3)
Round
Rk (7)

G34

G38

Fort Grey Tr (21)

Airport

(6)

Gd
Hanois
(13)

(1·8)

G37

Apex Hd

096°

House

Hayes Rk
(1)

G36

(1₅)
(1₂)

(3)

Pezeries Pt

120°

Hanois
Fl(2)13s33m20M
Horn(2)

Beacon Rk

1₅

1₅

Pleinmont Tr

Portelet
Hbr

See plan

(1₅)

0·3

Pleinmont Pt
Mast 2F.R

350°

Torteval (105)

L'Angle Tr

G32

093°

Herpin Rk
(1·5)

(3·3)

Les Tielle

German Tr
La Corbière

La Roc

G33

(2₁)

Tas de Pois
d'Aval (13)
Molière

G31

Bassière or
Pleinmont Ledge

(1₈)

(1₂)
(1₂)
Les
Kaines
d'Amont

Les Sept
Boues
(4₉)

Les Sept
Boues

(1₈)

Grande
Lieuse

Les
Lieuses (4)

298°

49°
25'
N

P1

G30

G35

G29

010°

**GUERNSEY
SOUTH COAST**

Depths in Metres

N

N

28'

27'

26'

24'

23'

43'   42'   41'   40'   39'   2°38'W   36'

42

For detailed coverage see plan

Transit G25 282° – German tower near La Corbière over the lower tip of Pte de la Moie. This avoids the danger of the set onto Grunes de Jerbourg and is regarded by the pilots to be safer than the transit of 276° on Admiralty *807* which can be used with care if a visit to Saints Bay is intended.

The 6 miles of the south coast, most of which is deep close in, is formed by an impressive line of cliffs in which there are several attractive bays, not necessarily uncomfortable at HW and quiet at half tide down.

Jerbourg Point forms the eastern arm of a bay over ½M wide containing the inlets Saints Bay, Moulin Huet, and Petit Port. A pleasant anchorage may be found here with due regard to Mouillière (drying 8·5m), used as a local racing mark, and other rocks shown on Admiralty *807*. The beacon in Saints Bay, shown on Admiralty *807* and *808*, marked the entry of old telephone cables, now replaced by a fibre optics cable.

There are steps up the cliff in Moulin Huet bay and Petit Port and a path inland from

Photo G26

Saints Bay (see Photo G26 – Saints Bay).

Transit G25 passes close to Baleine Rock (drying 0·9m) 500m SSW of Icart Point. If intending to enter Icart Bay with insufficient water over Baleine, when Icart Point bears north, turn to port and take:

Transit G27 281° – L'Angle German tower over the 'V' of Corbière. The photo shows Tas de Pois d'Aval (Gull Rock, height 13m) off Pleinmont Point and, to the left, Rousse de Moye (drying 6·1m) in front of Grande Lieuse (drying 7·9m).

Icart Bay is over ½M wide with Fourquie de la Moye (drying 3·3m) in the middle of the entrance.

To avoid the Fourquie locate the Martello tower in Petit Bôt Bay and steer in on:

Transit G28 353° with the tower just open of the point, coming to anchor in 3m east of the transit.

South of La Corbière lie a group of rocks some of which dry, including Les Lieuses (drying 4m), Les Sept Boues (drying 4·9m) and Grande Lieuse (drying 7·9m). The Guernsey pilots describe a passage, not included in this book, passing inside Les Sept Boues and continuing inshore of Les Kaines d'Amont.

The following transits will pass outside Les Lieuses and Les Kaines d'Amont to approach Pleinmont Point.

If not intending to visit Icart Bay, when Icart Point bears north, steer out on 262° to point P1 on the plan, page 43.

After visiting Icart Bay, come out to the point P2, where Transits G27 and G28 cross, and steer 253° for point P1.

At P1, where:

Breast mark G29 037° – La Roche in line with valley crosses:

Transit G30 298° – Hanois light open to the left of Tas de Pois d'Aval, steer on Transit G30 298° to approach Pleinmont Point.

On approaching Tas de Pois d'Aval (Gull Rock) leave it 200m to starboard to clear outliers to the south and southwest.

(Grade EC)

Rocquaine Bay is encumbered with rocks, one in the south being named Beacon Rock after the survey vessel which discovered it the hard way. Therefore, before turning north into Rocquaine Bay, it is well to make a start in identifying some of the rocks that will be used as marks.

From position 49°25'·4N 2°40'·17W:

Transit G31 332° – Round Rock (height 7m) will be open to the left of Herpin Rock (height 1·5m) and, looking east:

Bearing G32 093° La Corbière Tower will appear well open of Tas de Pois d'Aval and over Les Kaines d'Aval (drying 3·3m), barely visible in the photo to the right of a Tas de Pois outlier.

With Round Rock positively identified, steer 300° and look for the west head of Les Trois Pères (height 7m). When it is closing on Round Rock, take:

Bearing G32

Transit G33 350° – West head of Les Trois Pères in line with east side of Round Rock.

This transit passes over a 4·6m ridge and leaves close to starboard a rock with only 1·5m over it which can be avoided by easing to port so that Round Rock obscures the west head of Les Trois Pères.

On this transit, Nipple Rock (drying 8·5m) is seen to the right of Round Rock with Black Rock (drying 8·8m) and Lihou Island further to the right. Identify Saddle Rock on the skyline of Lihou Island and, when it is over Black Rock, take:

Transit G34 023° – Saddle Rock x Black Rock.

The Transit G33 passes close to a rock drying 0·9m, one of two to the east of Percée (height 1·8m), before the change to G34 and, when Hayes Rock (height 1m) is abeam to port, the west head of Les Trois Pères must be opened its width to the right of Round Rock.

Those familiar with the passage may use the transit on Admiralty *807*, which passes clear of the rock drying 0·9m. This is:

Transit G35 010°– Outer rock west of Lihou Island over the right-hand edge of Nipple Rock. However it is hard on a first visit to identify the outer rock.

Beacon Rock is waiting should the transit be missed.

Once Transit G34 is acquired, Portelet Harbour or an anchorage off Torquetil Rock (1m high) may be visited, or one can proceed north and out to the northwest.

PORTELET HARBOUR 49°26'·3N 2°39'·8W

This harbour dries and has two walls which cover at HW (see air photo page 48). There is an anchorage in 6m (sand) north of Pezeries Point and one can anchor and remain afloat NW of the small boat moorings.

With Round Rock abeam to port, identify Apex House, preferably with binoculars, and when:

Breast mark G36 245° – Hanois LtHo to the left of Round Rock, turn to starboard onto:

Transit G37 096° – Apex House x the left-hand wall of Fort Grey.

The marks for entering the anchorage are Torteval church spire and a conspicuous house with a red roof and white gable on the left among a group of bungalows (both arrowed in G37).

Enter, with attention to soundings, on:

Transit G38 120° – Torteval Spire x white gabled house.

Photo G39 shows the transit (170°) on Admiralty *807* which can only be used at HW as it crosses two rocky patches.

Portelet drying harbour

Photo G39

Transit 170° on Admiralty 807 for Portelet Harbour

TORQUETIL ROCK ANCHORAGE

With Nipple Rock abeam to port look for Torquetil Rock (height 1m and inconspicuous at LW), and Cacquerau House with a square tower and white flagstaff, half hidden in trees on the skyline.

Steer in on:

Transit G40 065° –Cacquerau House in line with left-hand end of Torquetil Rock.

This course passes over a 0·3m patch which would present a hazard at LWS and might be avoided by borrowing to port with the house open north, twice the width of the rock.

Anchor in 4m on the transit 400m from the rock.

Torquetil Rock

Transit G40

If the intention is to circumnavigate the island and the weather is settled, anchor off Portelet Harbour or Tortequil Rock and leave the next morning, aiming to arrive off Grande Havre at low water in order to see the rocks!

ROCQUAINE BAY TO BEAUCETTE, BY NORTHWEST COAST
(Grade EC all the way)

Chart
Admiralty *807*

Seven miles visibility is required, a calm sea with no swell and a reliable engine are essential for a first visit. The last circumnavigation made by the editor was in a summer heat haze. The distant marks were only identifiable (with binoculars) because they had been seen on previous occasions.

LEAVING ROCQUAINE BAY BY THE NORTHWEST PASSAGE
From Portelet Harbour or the Torquetil Rock anchorage, regain Transit G34 – Saddle Rock x Black Rock and proceed on 023°, looking astern for:

Round Rock   Nipple Rock

Transit G41 216° – Round Rock to the left of Nipple Rock.

Turn to starboard and follow this stern transit, leaving Black Rock (drying 8·8m) and Perron (drying 3·4m) 100m to port, with a drying rock 100m to starboard.

At this stage it is to be hoped that Perron is exposed as the stern transit G43 to leave the bay will touch the rock. As a precaution continue on G41 until:

Transit G42 142° – Torteval Spire over the clear patch of sand to the left of Fort Grey.

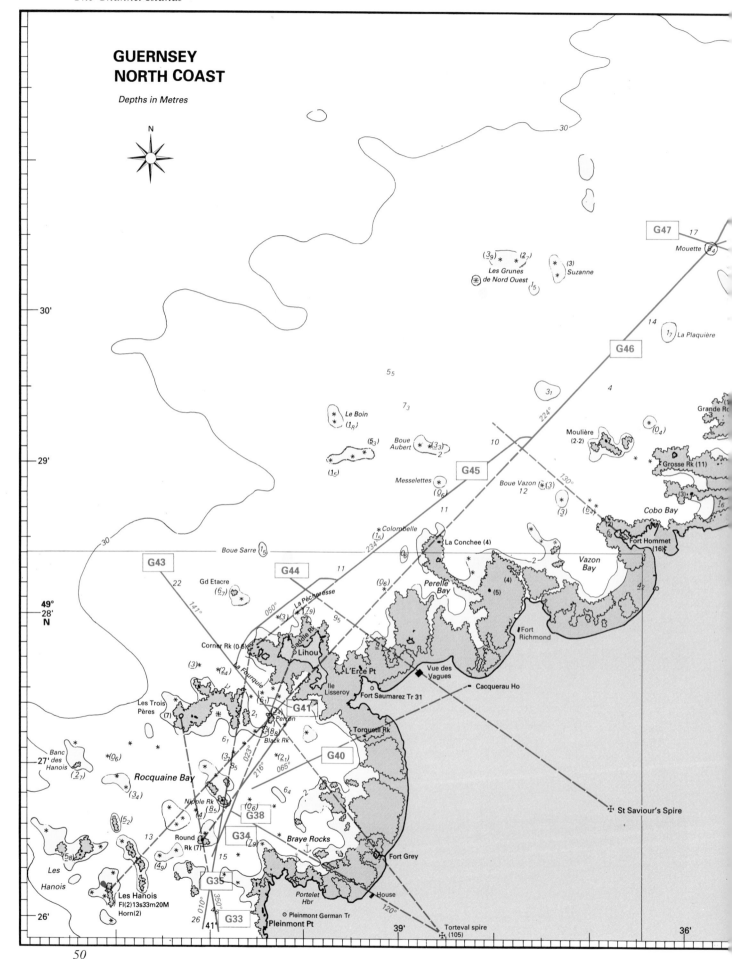

GUERNSEY
NORTH COAST

Depths in Metres

N

G47 17
Mouette (9₄)

(3₉) * (2₇)   (3)
Les Grunes *   * Suzanne
⊕ de Nord Ouest
(5)

14
1₇ La Plaquière

G46

30'

5₅

7₃   3₁   4

Le Boin   Moulière
* (2·2)   * (0₄)
(1₈)
Boue   Grande R
(5₃)   Aubert * (3₃)   Grosse Rk (11)
*   2   * (3)
(1₅)   Boue Vazon (*(3)   (3)

29'
G45   12
Messelettes *   (3)   (6₄)
(0₆)   Cobo Bay
11
* Colombelle   6₄
(1₅)   La Conchee (4)   Fort Hommet
30   * 2   (16)
Boue Sarre (1₅)   (0₆)   Vazon
Bay
G43   11   Perelle
234°   Bay (4)   4₂
22   (0₆)   (5)
Gd Etacre   G44   *
(6₇)   La Pécheresse
141°   050°   Fort
*(3) *(7₉)   9₅   Richmond
49°
28'   Saddle Rk
N   Corner Rk (0·6)   Lihou   L'Erée Pt
(3) *   *(2₄)   Vue des
La Fourquie   Ile Lisseroy   Vagues
Les Trois   (6₁)   Fort Saumarez Tr 31   Cacquerau Ho
Pères (7)   2₁   G41
Percon   Torquetil Rk
(8₈)
6₁   Black Rk   G40
Banc   *(0₆)   (3)   8₅   *(2₁)
27'   des   216°   065°
Hanois   (2₇)   Rocquaine Bay   6₄
(3₄)
Nipple Rk
(5₂)   (4)   8₅   (0₆)   St Saviour's Spire
G38
13   Round   G34   Braye Rocks
(4₉)   Rk (7)   (7₉)   Fort Grey
Les   15
5₈   G35
Hanois   House
Les Hanois   Portelet   120°
Fl(2)13s33m20M   Hbr
Horn(2)   010°   350°   Torteval spire
26'   26   4₁   Pleinmont German Tr   (105)
G33   Pleinmont Pt   39'   36'

50

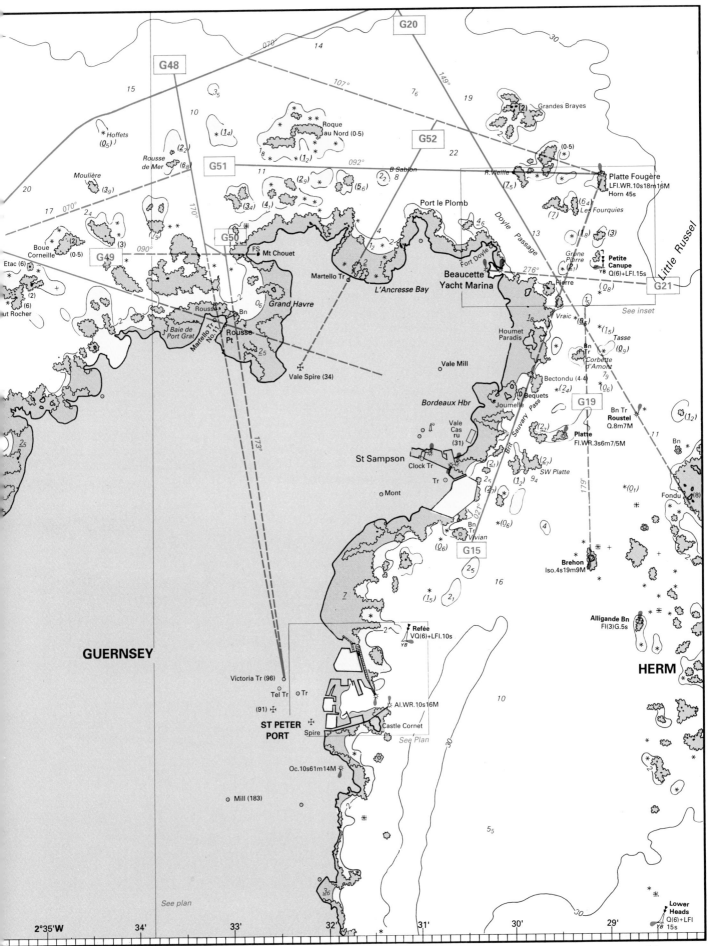

G20

G48

G52

G51

14

070°

15

107°

7₆

149°

19

(2) Grandes Brayes

30

3₅

10

* Hoffets
(0₅))

(1₄)

Roque
au Nord (0·5)

22

092°

(0·5)
(*)

Platte Fougère
LFl.WR.10s18m16M
Horn 45s

Moulière

Rousse
de Mer

(2₂)

(6₈)

1₈

(1₂)

11

(2₉)

B Sablon

2₂ 8

R. Weille

(7₅)

(6₄)

(7)

Les Fourquies

Little Russel

20

(3₉)

(3₄)

(4₁)

(5₆)

Port le Plomb

4₆

Doyle Passage

13

(1₈)

(3)

17

070°

2₄

G50

4

1₂

2

Fort Doyle

Grûne
Pierre

(2₁)

276°

G21

Boue
Corneille

(2)

(0·5)

090°

G49

*

FS

Mt Chouet

2₇

2

1₇

Beaucette
Yacht Marina

Pierre

(0₈)

(1₅)

See inset

Etac (6)

Martello Tr

L'Ancresse Bay

Vraic

(0₅)

(1₅)

Tasse

(2)

(6)

Rousse

Bn

0₆

Grand Havre

Houmet
Paradis

1₈

Bn
Tr

(0₉)

Corbette
d'Amont

ut Rocher

Baie de
Port Grat

Martello Tr
No.1 Tr

Rousse
Pt

2

2₅

Bectondu (4·4)

7₉

(2₄)

(0₆)

2₅

Vale Mill

Vale Spire (34)

G19

Bn Tr
Roustel
Q.8m7M

(1₂)

173°

Bordeaux Hbr

Bequets

Joumelle

(2₇)

Platte
Fl.WR.3s6m7/5M

11

Bn

Vale
Cas
ru
(31)

Brit Sauvary Pass

(2₇)

SW Platte

(0₁)

St Sampson

Clock Tr

Tr

(2₁)

9₄

Fondu

(8)

Mont

2₅

(1₂)

⁂

(2₇)

02°

Bn
Tr
Vivian

(0₆)

4

Brehon
Iso.4s19m9M

⁂

+

+

(0₆)

G15

2₅

16

GUERNSEY

7

(1₅)

2₁

Alligande Bn
Fl(3)G.5s

⁂

HERM

Refée
VQ(6)+LFl.10s

2

Victoria Tr (96)

Tel Tr

Tr

10

(91) ⁂

Al.WR.10s16M

ST PETER
PORT

Spire

Castle Cornet

See Plan

30

Oc.10s61m14M

Mill (183)

⁂

5₅

See plan

3₆

30

Lower
Heads
Q(6)+LFl
15s

2°35'W

34'

33'

32'

31'

30'

29'

Turn sharply to port and take this stern transit to pass Perron and acquire as a new stern transit:

Transit G43 141° – Torteval Spire over the left-hand edge of Fort Grey.

G43 leads out through a gap less than 200m wide between La Fourquie (drying 6·1m) to starboard and an isolated drying rock and reef to port. The photo G43 shows La Fourquie to the left and the southern part of Perron just emerging to the right of the transit. This transit will take you right out to sea.

When entering Rocquaine Bay from the northwest, hold the Transit G43 until La Fourquie, which is steep-to, is passed and then, to avoid Perron, take Transit G42 with the spire over the patch of sand to the left of the fort. Turn onto Transit G41 immediately it has been acquired in order to avoid the drying rock SE of Perron.

CONTINUING TO THE NORTHEAST

Northeast of Lihou Island are a number of bays with small fishing boats on moorings and sandy beaches that are worth a visit. These are not described in this book but entry is possible by referring to chart Admiralty *807*.

Leave the stern transit G43 and, rounding Corner Rock (height 0·6m) at a distance of at least 200m, steer 050° for 0·6M, leaving a rock drying 3m and La Pécheresse (drying 7·9m) to starboard and passing inshore of Grande Etacré (drying 6·7m).

In this area the courses will pass inshore of a number of isolated rocks, the first being Colombelle (drying 1·5m).

With La Pécheresse 400m to the south, steer to the east. The breast mark, if it can be identified, being:

Breast mark G44 125° x St Saviours Spire x Vue des Vagues, a red-roofed house with two dormer windows.

Continue east until:

Transit G45 234° – La Pécheresse covering Corner Rock. The photo shows La Pécheresse well open to the right of Corner Rock for easy identification but the two rocks must be in line to clear the approximate position of the wreck of *Prosperity*, lost some years ago with all hands. Her engine can still be seen on the end of the rocks off La Conchée.

Steer 056° with G45 as a stern transit for 1½M until Fort Hommet bears 130°. If entering either Vazon or Cobo Bay, avoid Boue Vazon (drying 3m). If proceeding northeast, the next stern transit, with distant marks, will lead outside Grand Saut Rocher (6m). The passages inshore will be left to the locals.

Transit G46 224° – Les Hanois lighthouse x a small, conspicuous group of rocks showing over the shingle ridge joining Lihou Island and Ile Lissroy. In the photo the lighthouse is to the left of the group of rocks.

Steer 044° on this stern transit for 2½M, observing fishing buoys to monitor the tidal set and identifying marks on shore as well as rocks named on chart *807*.

Note that this course passes over Moulrette (depth 8·4m) and the sea must be calm, with no swell.

L'Etac (height 6m) is a conspicuous rock on the south side of the channel for entry into Baie de Port Grat (see Admiralty *807*) which can also be used to enter the inshore channel to Grand Havre.

Transit G47 108° – Martello tower on Rousse Point between Vale mill and Vale church. (Note the three St Sampson chimneys.)

Passing this transit it is possible, at low water to navigate with caution, steering about 070° with no marks, through a wide channel and arrive southeast of the conspicuous Rousse de Mer (drying 6·8m) in preparation for entry to Grand Havre. It is however considered safer to take this passage when travelling west.

Continuing on the stern transit G46, after passing G47 as a breast mark, alter to port and put the Les Hanois lighthouse on the left-hand edge of Lihou Island in order to clear the 'unexamined' shallows off Hoffets (drying 0·5m).

When clear to the north of Hoffets, come round to the east to pick up:

Transit G48 170° – Victoria Tower open to the left of Martello tower No. 11 on Rousse Point.

If a visit to Grand Havre is not intended, steer 070° to avoid the shallows north of Roque au Nord (height 0·5m) and search for Transit G20 149° – Roustel midway between Herm and Jethou. Follow this transit on 149° to enter the Doyle Passage (page 38) and return to Beaucette or St Peter Port.

Since the old Roustel Bn Tr has been replaced by an inconspicuous framed structure, it may be invisible from this distance, in which case take Corbette d'Amont (see photo page 37) halfway between Jethou and Herm on 146° as an alternative. This will take you as far as Beaucette, giving time to identify Roustel.

GRAND HAVRE

From a distance it is impossible to identify the end of Rousse Point and the 171° transit shown on Admiralty *807* cannot be used for entry.

However, for departure from Grand Havre:

Photo G48A shows the transit, with Victoria Tower over a long reddish-brown roof with Rousse above-water rock to the right.

To enter

Steer 170° on G48 and identify the Martello tower, flagstaff and fence on Mt Chouet (see G49). The German tower on Mt Chouet has collapsed but a bunker remains below the fence.

Photo G49 – Mount Chouet German bunker and flagstaff on 090°(not the required 095°).

When the fence and flagstaff bear 095°, steer 120° and identify the beacon on the end of Rousse Pier. When the beacon comes in line with Victoria Tower, steer into the bay on:

Transit G50 173° – Victoria Tower x beacon on Rousse Pier.

Victoria Tower

Anchor on soundings with reference to tidal level and to Admiralty *807*.

LEAVING GRAND HAVRE AND PROCEEDING EAST

1. Either go out holding the stern transit G50 with care, as a drying 0·9m rock is close to the east, crossing to G48 when the Mt Chouet flagstaff bears 095° and, passing Rousse de Mer (drying 6·8m), turn east to steer on Platte Fougère when it bears 107°.
2. Or if it is low water and the rocks drying 1m and 1·2m south of Silleuse (drying 6·4m) can be detected by the disturbed water surrounding them, as Rousse de Mer approaches the port beam, turn onto 092° and follow:

Transit G51 092° – Platte Fougère over Roque Vieille (drying 7·5m) with Grande Amfroque well open to the south.

This passage is narrow, with distant marks, and passes close to the two drying rocks south of Silleuse. If Roque Vieille is not clearly visible at this distance, those familiar with the passage may steer 092°, holding Rousse de Mer carefully on the reciprocal bearing of 272° until the transit is confirmed. Others may prefer to use it only when travelling east–west.

Photo G51A shows two views of Rousse de Mer in hazy conditions.

Proceeding east, hold G51 until the Doyle Passage is reached, then follow Transit G20 for Beaucette Marina or on to St Peter Port.

WESTWARDS FROM GRAND HAVRE

1. Either go out using G50, G49 and G48 in reverse and acquire G46 when it is safe to do so.
2. Or go out on G50, G49 and G48 until Rousse de Mer (drying 6·8m) 200m distant, bears 290°. Then steer 250° through the passage between Moulière (drying 3·9m) and the group of rocks containing Roque Noire (height 3m) to join Transit G46.

L'ANCRESSE BAY

This wide, sandy bay is situated to the east of Grand Havre and one, clear transit may be used for entry.

Reference to Admiralty *807* suggests that there are few isolated rocks.

Transit G52 210° – Vale church x Martello tower No. 7.

Anchor afloat or take the ground on sand if winds are steady from the south.

Facilities

None are given for this passage as it is assumed that the yacht will be fully provisioned and fuelled.

Herm and Jethou

Rosière Steps landing 49°28'·00N 2°27'·13W

Herm, rich in archaeological remains, was the pre-Christian burial-ground for Guernsey and for continental burials, as spirits could not cross water and interfere with the living.

Sadly, in the 19th century, tons of granite were quarried from the island and many of the capstones, lying on the surface, were easy to pick up and export to London.

The chapel is dedicated to St Tugual, one of the many Britons who crossed the channel to escape the invading Saxons and is reputed to have founded the City of Tréguier in Brittany. A small monastic community occupied the island until the Reformation when it became a refuge for 400 Catholics until they were expelled (possibly from this earth?) by Calvinists.

The island then became a hunting reserve for the Governor of Guernsey. Sir Thomas Leighton stocked it with deer, pheasants, rabbits and a breed of swans.

After 1821 when it was exploited for its granite, the population grew in ten years from 37 to nearly 300 and a harbour was built for vessels of a fair size to enter and load the stone. By 1880 the stone trade had declined and the population had fallen to 31.

From the end of the 19th century until the Second World War Herm was let by the British government to various individuals including the Prussian Prince Blucher von Wahlstatt who introduced wallabies and the novelist Compton Mackenzie who took the lease in 1920 before moving to the smaller island of Jethou in 1923.

After the Second World War the States purchased Herm from the British Government for the people of Guernsey for recreation and leased it to Major Wood and his family who have developed it and are maintaining it in excellent condition.

Jethou is Crown property, leased to a private tenant, and landing is forbidden.

Facilities

The Tenant of Herm welcomes visiting yachtsmen but requests that they seek permission if they wish to stay in the harbour overnight. This is available without charge from the administration office at the harbour.

Herm Harbour is a good half-tide harbour, busy with passenger launches and very crowded with Guernsey boats at weekends but usually with plenty of space on other days for visiting yachts to anchor or moor to buoys. Yachts with legs or bilge keels can dry out on the beach on the east side of the harbour where there are chain trots to which drying out boats may moor fore and aft.

A freshwater tap, toilets, hot water showers, shop with most basic provisions, gift shops, rubbish collection and public telephones are all available near the harbour.

The island is kept scrupulously clean, with three restaurants and bars, Belvoir and Shell Beach cafés, one hotel, self-catering accommodation and camp sites with tents provided.

The island of Herm, just over 1M long, is at the centre of a long reef stretching from Grande Amfroque in the NE, through the Humps, Herm, Jethou with its satellites Crevichon and Grande Fauconnière, La Platte, Les Ferrières, Les Barbées and down to the Lower Heads, marked by the Lower Heads buoy (S card).

Many beacons on the west side mark the channels through the reef from the Little Russel to the Big Russel. There are fewer dangers on the east side and only one beacon (Noire Pute), and a N card buoy (Fourquies).

Charts

Admiralty *2669, 3654, 808*. Photocopies of the older charts *262a, 262b* may be obtainable from the Hydrographic Office but they do not overlap sufficiently to show the whole area on either. The new Admiralty charts are based on European Datum. Imray *C33A*

Lights

These are included for local yachtsmen. Visitors are not encouraged to approach Herm at night.
1. **Brehon Tower** 49°28'·3N 2°29'·2W Iso.4s19m9M Beacon on round tower
2. **Tautenay** 49°30'·2N 2°26'·7W Q(3)WR.6s7m7/6M Black and white beacon 050°-W-215°-R-050°
3. **Alligande beacon** 49°27'·9N 2°28'·7W Fl(3)G.5s Black pole, orange 'A' topmark
4. **Epec beacon** 49°28'·0N 2°27'·8W Fl.G.3s Green pole, black 'E' topmark
5. **Vermerette beacon** 49°28'·2N 2°27'·7W Fl(2)Y.5s Yellow pole, orange 'V' (filled in white)
6. **Percée Passage, Gate Rock** 49°27'·5N 2°34'·8W Q(9)15s W card beacon
7. **Noire Pute** 49°28'·3N 2°24'·9W Fl(2)WR.15s8m6M On rock. 220°-W-040°-R-220°
8. **Fourquies** 49°27'·4N 2°26'·4W ⁂ card buoy Q
9. **Lower Heads** 49°25'·9N 2°28'·5W ⁋ card buoy Q(6)+LFl.15s.

Tidal levels referred to chart datum

St Peter Port 49°27'N 2°31'W MHWS 9·3m MHWN 7·0m MLWN 3·6m MLWS 1·5m MTL 5·3m

Tidal streams

Along the Big Russel side of Herm and the Humps the stream runs nearly the same as in the Big Russel itself.

On the west side of Herm the flood stream in the Little Russel meets a constriction north of Brehon and, when the sand west of Herm is covered, an eddy forms which initially runs south along the shore, through the Rosière anchorage, to maintain the SE stream in the Percée Passage and south of Herm into the Big Russel.

Effectively in the Percée Passage the stream runs SE for nine hours, starting at about LW, and NW

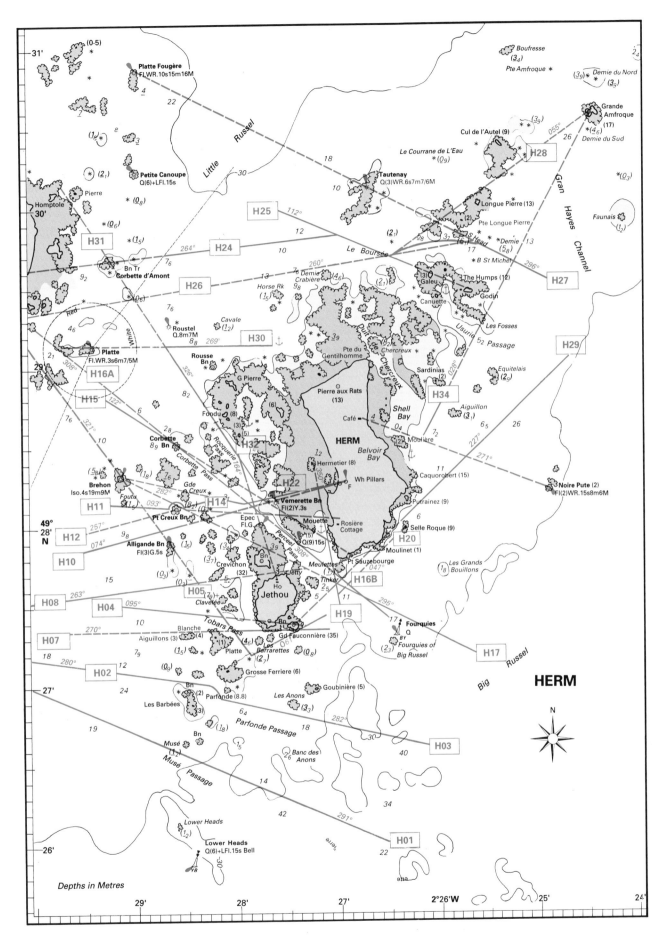

31'

(0·5)

Platte Fougère
Fl.WR.10s15m16M
4
22

Russel

Little

Boufresse
(3₄)
Pte Amfroque *

Demie du Nord
(3₉)
(3₉)

2₄

*(3₉)

Grande Amfroque
(17)
*(4₆)
Demie du Sud

055°

26

(1₈) * e
* 3

Petite Canoupe
Q(6)+LFl.15s

18

30

Cul de l'Autel (9)

Le Courrane de L'Eau
*(0₉)

(3₉)

Gran

Hayes Channel

296°

* (2₁)

Pierre *

(0₈)

Tautenay
Q(3)WR.6s7m7/6M
10

*

Longue Pierre (13)

(2₁)
Pte Longue Pierre

*(0₃)

Faunais
(1₂)

Homptole
30'

*(0₆)

H31

*(1₅)

H25 112°

H24 264°

7₆

12

10

Le Boursée

13

7₆ **Demie Crabière**
9₈

Horse Rk
(1₅)

(4₆)

260°

S Head
2₈ 3₇ (6₁)

Demie (5₈) 13

* B St Michel
17

The Humps (12)

H27

Corbette d'Amont
Bn Tr

H26

9₂

*(0₅)

7₆

Cavale
(1₂)

Roustel
Q.8m7M
8₈ 269°

H30 ⚓

(3₉)

(2₁)

Galeu (3₂)

Canuette

Godin

Les Fosses

Usurie

5₂ Passage

Equitelais
(2₉)

H29

Red
4₆

White

21

Platte
Fl.WR.3s6m7/5M

308°

H16A

122°

H15

321°

Rousse
Bn

82

G Pierre

6

Pte du Gentilhomme

(3₂)

Chercreux

Sardinias (2)

H34

Aiguillon
(3₁)

26

H32

Pierre aux Rats
(13)

Shell Bay

Café 4

Moulière

04

7₂

6₅

6

HERM

Belvoir Bay

227°

271°

Noire Pute (2)
Fl(2)WR.15s8m6M

7₆

6

Fondu (8)

(3)

(5)

Corbette
Bn
8₉

2₈

Roquerie Pass

(6)

164°

(1₂)

Hermetier (8)

150°

F

Wh Pillars

11

Caquorobert (15)

Putrainez (9)

H22

H14

(5₈)

Brehon
Iso.4s19m9M

(1₈)

7₆

093°

Gde Creux

(8₂)

282°

Vemerette Bn
Fl(2)Y.3s

Mouette

Rosière Cottage

Selle Roque (9)

H20

H11

Foutu
(1₅)

257°

Pt Creux Bn

Epec
Fl.G.

308°

(5)

Q(9)15s

Moulinet (1)

49° 28' N

H12

074°

9₈

Alligande Bn
Fl(3)G.5s

(1₅)

(3₄)

Percee Pass

047°

Pt Sauzebourge

H16B

Les Grands Bouillons
(1₈)

H10

(3₇)

Crevichon (32)

Meulettes
(1₁)

Tinkar
2₅

5

295°

H05

(0₃)

(0₂)

Bn

Jethou

Ho

Jetty

H19

11

Fourquies
Q
BY

17

H08 263°

(7₆)+
Clavelée

5

H04 095°

Tobars Pass

10

Blanche
(4)

Bn

Gd Fauconnière (35)

Fourquies of Big Russel
(2₃)

H17

Russel

H07 270°

Aiguillons (3)

Platte

Les Barrarettes
(2₁)

(0₈)

Big

HERM

18 280°

7₉

(1₅)

(4₆)

6₁

H02

12

(0₉)

Grosse Ferriere (6)

N

24

Bn
Parfonde (8.8)
(2)

Les Anons

Goubinière (5)

Les Barbées

(3₃)

(3₃)

Bn

H03

6₄

19

Bn

Parfonde Passage

18

282°

(1₈)

Musé
(1₂)

(1₅)

Banc des Anons
2₆

30

40

Musé Passage

14

34

42 291°

Lower Heads
(1₂)

Yerre

aha

H01

22

Lower Heads
Q(6)+LFl.15s Bell
YB

30

Depths in Metres

29' 28' 27' 2°26'W 25' 24'

for three hours, after a period of slack, from HW+3.

In the Neck of Jethou, which is awash at half tide, it will always run east and can reach 6 knots at springs.

In Le Boursée Channel north of the Humps the tide runs at from 5 to 6 knots. In direction it tends to follow the channel but there is a danger of a cross set, and the flow must be monitored when using the passage.

Pilotage

Pilotage in the area mainly involves the channels running between the Little and Big Russel north and south of Herm and these will be described first, passing west to east and starting at the south. It is advisable to plot the transits on the navigational chart in use and reverse the directions when passing east to west.

The photographs on page 71 show some of the marks and beacons surrounding Herm.

The Lower Heads S card buoy[9] 49°25'·9N 2°28'·5W marks the southern extent of the reef. Between the Lower Heads (drying 1·2m) 300m north of the buoy and the Musé (drying 1·2m) is a channel   M wide:

THE MUSE PASSAGE (12m) (Grade M)

The Musé beacon (yellow with a red 'M' topmark) is mounted on Demie Ferrière rock (drying 4·9m) about 200m ENE of the Musé rock.

To pass through from west to east, take as a stern transit:

Victoria Tower

Transit H01 291° – Victoria Tower over the north end of Castle Cornet. With this stern transit the Musé rock will be left 200m to port and the beacon 300m to port.

THE PARFONDE PASSAGE (2·8m) (Grade M)

This passage, 200m wide, is not difficult and passes between Les Barbées (2m) to the south (marked by a yellow beacon with a red can topmark) and rocks drying 3m to the north. The Parfonde rock (drying 8·8m and so usually exposed) lies 300m to the east of Les Barbées.

A substitute is given for the transit on Admiralty *808* since Sark church can no longer be identified. Coming from St Peter Port, take as a stern transit:

Transit H02 280° – Telephone Link Tower, with its two white dishes (shown as TV Tr on 808), just to the left (south) of the Castle breakwater LtHo. On this transit the spire of St James' church is over the lighthouse and the square tower of Elizabeth College is to the left of the Telephone Link Tower.

After leaving Les Barbées beacon 100m to starboard (note the head drying 1·2m 100m WNW of the beacon), alter to starboard to avoid Parfonde and ensure that the tidal stream does not take you onto Les Anons (drying 3·3m) which lie 0·43M ESE of Parfonde.

Take as a stern transit:

Transit H03 282° – Victoria Tower just to the right (north) of Les Barbées beacon. Hold this stern transit for 1M to clear between Les Anons and the Banc des Anons (2·6m over).

TOBARS PASSAGE (5·0m) (Grade EC)

This passage is much used by local boats but visitors should be sure of the marks before attempting it.

The passage is entered 200m north of the above-water rocks Aiguillons (height 3m) and Blanche (height 4m) whitened by bird lime. 300m east of Blanche an extensive plateau of rocks (La Platte), with two above-water heads (height 1m) in the middle, stretches further north and should be left 100m or more to starboard.

Clavelée, with three heads all drying 7·9m and incorrectly shown on Admiralty *808* as one drying 3·7m, lies 300m north of La Platte. Drying heads extend 150m south of Clavelée and are left to port.

The next hazard is a group of rocks, Les Barrarettes (drying 4·3m and 3·9m), close south of Jethou and preferably left to port, after which Grande Fauconnière (height 35m) is left 100m to port, avoiding rocks drying up to 0·8m to the south.

The transits are:

Transit H04 095° – Grande Fauconnière on the south slope of Jethou with the Bec du Nez of Sark just obscured behind the slope. On this transit Sark is often hidden in the haze. The 090° transit shown on Admiralty *808*, with Bec du Nez well open, passes rather too close to La Platte.

When about 400m short of Jethou turn to starboard and take as a stern transit:

Transit H05 321° – Vale Mill Tower on with the left side of Brehon Tower. In the photo, Alligande beacon is in front of Brehon with a rock SW of Clavelée showing to the right. If Vale Mill is obscured by haze, put Alligande in the middle of Brehon.

When the beacon on the summit of Grande Fauconnière bears 055°, Noire Pute (height 2m) with a beacon (photo H06) should open from behind Grande Fauconnière. When

Photo H06

Noire Pute bears 061° steer to hold it on this bearing, leaving Grande Fauconnière 100m to port.

After experience in these waters it is possible, when travelling east–west towards St Peter Port, to pass north of Les Barrarettes, in a passage 50m wide and 2·6m deep, after passing Grande Fauconnière by taking:

Transit H07 270° – The green spire of St Joseph's church just open of the north face of Blanche. Photo H07A shows the transit near HW with part of La Platte showing front left.

Photo H07B, taken near LW shortly after passing Grande Fauconnière, shows the transit with part of Les Barrarettes on the left and La Platte fully exposed and stretching either side of Blanche. A launch is passing through on the extreme right of the picture.

When Transit H05 321° comes on, turn to starboard onto 321° to clear La Platte and then take Transit H04 095° as a stern transit to pass out north of Blanche.

THE NECK OF JETHOU (drying 5m)
(Grade EC)

This 'high-water' passage between Crevichon and Jethou may be taken in either direction, subject to a reliable prediction of tide level, and remembering that the stream will be setting east.

Transit H08 263°   Crossing from St Peter Port, the stern transit is:

Transit H08 263° – The green spire of St Joseph's church over the White Rock lighthouse beside the port signal station.

Take this transit when 300m south of Alligande beacon and, taking account of the tidal set, hold it, passing close south of rocks drying 5·2m, 600m from the neck.

With Crevichon and Jethou abeam on either side, identify the root of the sloping 'jetty' on Jethou, most of which will be submerged (see photo H09).

When 60m from the jetty, turn sharply to port and steer 030° for the Percée beacon (see photo page 63), with careful attention to the stream, to enter the Percée Passage.

Photo H09

ALLIGANDE PASSAGE (0·5m) (Grade M)

This passage is much used and is the most direct route from St Peter Port (known as Town) to Herm Harbour when there is enough water to approach the harbour.

Note that when Vermerette beacon's rock (drying 4·3m) is covered, there should be about 1m of water at the end of the quay.

Leaving Alligande beacon (green with an 'A' topmark and lit) 200m to starboard, identify Vermerette beacon (yellow with a 'V' topmark and lit) and the white patch on the end of Herm Quay, with the aid of the buildings on the ridge behind.

Take:

Transit H10 074° – Vermerette beacon x white patch on end of quay. This transit will lead into the Corbette/ Percée Passage.

To reach the harbour (above half tide), when 200m from Vermerette beacon, turn to port and come onto Transit H22 (page 64) to proceed towards the quay.

Note that the drying area north of Vermerette is sand and stones and not rocky as shown on Admiralty *807* and *808* but there are rocks to the south. The drying 4·3m symbol should be bracketed as it refers to Vermerette rock.

CREUX PASSAGE (3m) (Grade EC)

This is the low-water passage from Town to Herm and starts with a transit that will only just clear Foutu (drying 1·5m), 300m south of Brehon Tower:

Transit H11 093°

Rosière Cottage

Petit Creux Bn

Transit H11 093° – Rosière Cottage above Rosière Steps on Herm open to the right of Petit Creux beacon (orange-red with a 'C' topmark). The cottage should be further open than in the photo.

When 100m from Petit Creux beacon, turn to port and do a 'handrail' round it, leaving it 60m to starboard until, looking astern:

Transit H12 257° – Victoria Tower seen to the right of Petit Creux beacon. In the photograph Victoria Tower is to the left of Petit Creux and, on the ebb, it is better to have the green spire of St Joseph's church (arrowed) just to the left of the beacon.

After 400m take as a second stern transit and allowing once more for the ebb:

Transit H14 282° – Brehon Tower to the right of the highest part of Grande Creux.

This course joins the Corbette Passage.

CORBETTE PASSAGE (Grade M)

There are 2m or less between Vermerette and Epec beacons where silting has been reported.

Corbette passage can be used as a direct route from St Sampson to Sark as it leads into the Percée Passage and out south of Herm with no course alteration until clear, when the Fourquies buoy must be left to starboard.

Note that there are two rocks, Corbette d'Amont (drying 5·5m), with a yellow beacon tower NW of Roustel and Corbette de la Mare (drying 7·3m and marked by Corbette beacon on Admiralty *807* or *808*) with the beacon described below.

When at least 600m off to the NW, identify Corbette beacon (yellow with a white disc topmark as seen from the west) and take:

Transit H15 122° – Sauzebourge Point (on Herm) x Corbette de la Mare beacon. Vermerette beacon (yellow with a 'V' topmark and lit) and Mouette (height 5m) should be visible to the left of Corbette.

Corbette de la Mare rock is steep-to on the south side, so leaving it 30m to port, take as a stern transit:

Transit H16A 308° – Vale Mill building open twice its own width SW (to the left) of Corbette beacon with its red disc topmark as seen from the east.

At high water the rock is covered but the beacon is still conspicuous. Strong crosscurrents, especially on the flood, will set towards the rocks drying 6·7m shown on the plan, page 57.

Vale Mill

Transit H16A

After the Percée beacon (YBY and lit with an offset ⅃ card topmark and known locally as Gate Rock beacon as it is on Gate Rock) has been left to port, if the tide is right, a turn to port may be made across a sandbank with 0·3m over it and the conspicuous Mouette (height 5m) rock left to port to approach Herm Harbour which dries 3·5m or the Rosière Steps landing off which 4m may be found.

PERCEE PASSAGE (3·4m) (Grade M) Pronounced 'Per-she'.

For a first visit to Herm, the simple approach is from the SE.

However should the tidal set be ignored, there may well be an increase in the quota of yachts acquired in the summer months by Tinker (drying 2·5m) on the SW of the entrance or Meulettes (drying 1·7m) on the NE.

Passing through from the NW via the Corbette Passage, the Percée Passage, a continuation of the Corbette Passage, is entered at the line between Epec and Vermerette beacons and the stern Transit H16A 308° is held until clear to the SE.

For entry from the SE the same transit may be used but binoculars may be necessary to identify Corbette beacon.

Epec

Percée

Transit H16B 308° is the same as H16A but with Percée beacon on Gate Rock seen to the right and Epec beacon (green with 'E' topmark and lit) to the left.

If Corbette or Vale Mill cannot be seen, entry may be made clear south of Meulettes with:

Brehon

Fourquies buoy

Crevichon

Transit H17 295° – Brehon Tower well open to the north of Crevichon. Coming from Sark this transit may be acquired to pass north of Fourquies cardinal north buoy, with due allowance of tidal set. In the photo, Brehon is bearing 297° and the Fourquies buoy is seen to the north of this line.

Another transit for entry from the south which, with care, will clear Tinker to the east is:

Transit H18 327° (no photo) – Vermerette beacon open to the right of Percée beacon.

ROSIERE STEPS AND THE HARBOUR (Grade M)

In order to avoid Meulettes (drying 1·7m) when approaching Rosière Steps from the southeast keep:

Transit H19 350° – Hermetier open to the west of Rosière Steps.

When leaving, use the above as a stern transit and do not turn east until:

Transit H19

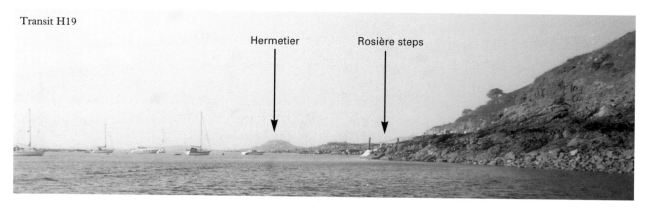

Breast mark H20 047° – Selle Roque (height 9m) is open south of Moulinet or Boue au Port (height 1m) as named on Admiralty 808.

The photo shows the double hump of Selle Roque over Moulinet but this line may pass too close to Meulettes.

Note that a 'Boue' is a rock that covers at the end (*bout* in modern French) of a reef, and Moulinet, which does not cover, is the local name for the above-water 'Boue au Port'.

Approaching or leaving Rosière Steps, the marks to clear east of Tinker (drying 2·5m), with due allowance for tidal set, are:

Transit H21 353° – Hermetier to the right of Mouette.

Do not go alongside Rosière Steps when the tide is running strongly as the yacht will be set heavily onto the piles.

Above half tide Herm Harbour (drying 3·5m) may be approached from the position where the Creux Passage joins the Corbette Passage, passing north of Vermerette beacon. The drying 4·3m symbol on Admiralty *808* north of Vermerette beacon refers to the rock itself which will be left 80m to starboard.

The transit is:

Transit H22 078° – Two white pillars about 2m high in line.

Photo H23 shows the harbour jetty which, at high water, is in constant use by the ferries. Note the wooden post with red top, to be left to port on entry.

LEAVING THE HARBOUR AT NIGHT (Grade EC)

The two white pillars are lit (F) at night and local yachts return to St Peter Port, when there is sufficient water, by leaving the quay on the 078° transit, rounding Vermerette beacon (Fl(2)Y.5s) and proceeding out through the Alligande Passage with one of the white lights on either side of Vermerette light.

H10 (page 61) shows the white pillars on either side of Vermerette.

Anchorage

The plan (page 57) shows the anchorage off Rosière Steps where yachts may remain afloat allowing passage for the ferries. When Vermerette rock is awash there is about 1m at the end of the jetty and the top landing at Rosière will cover about 20 minutes after Vermerette is covered.

With the drying area between Vermerette and the jetty covered, the southerly stream in the anchorage may reach 3 to 4 knots and, between HW −½ and +2 a standing wave can develop, especially in fresh SW winds, which makes it dangerous to use the dinghy, and an anchor watch may be necessary.

Below half tide the stream is less strong and as the sand uncovers the anchorage becomes a pool with no stream. Land in the dinghy, using Rosière Steps.

North of Herm

LE BOURSEE (10m) (Grade EC)

When taking this passage for the first time, visibility should be such that Platte Fougère lighthouse is clearly visible.

The passage is best taken west to east below half tide when the rocks are exposed. At times the easterly stream can be running at up to 8 knots, springs, and Boue St Michel, a pointed head just exposed at LWS, waits to add to the number of vessels that he has trapped.

The passage is entered 0·4M SW of Tautenay beacon tower, a truncated pyramid with black and white vertical stripes (see photos pages 67, 71).

Coming from St Peter Port or St Sampson, steer up the Little Russel passing Roustel on either side. Identify Corbette d'Amont yellow conical beacon and the conspicuous Vale

Transit H24 264°

Transit H24 264° – Vale Mill over Corbette d'Amont.

Mill and take as a stern transit:

Identify Godin (height 12m) and the smaller Galeu (height 3m) on the Humps. The next transit is:

Transit H25 112° – The highest point of Godin just to the left of the highest point of Galeu.

First option

Look for the next stern transit and, when 600m off Galeu take:

Transit H26 260° – Southernmost of the three power station chimneys over the north head of Demie Crabière (drying 4·6m).

Hold this stern transit with due allowance for tidal set and, with good visibility, identify the tall Platte Fougère lighthouse. When it comes close to Tautenay take as a stern transit:

Transit H27A 296° – Platte Fougère lighthouse to the left (south) of Tautenay beacon tower, appearing over the south head of Petite Longue Pierre. Photo: Derek Boyer.

Should Platte Fougère be hidden in haze, or obscured by the rocks as in the photo, it will be necessary to use Tautenay and the south head of Petite Longue Pierre in transit, and the south head must therefore be positively identified.

Hold this transit with care, in order to avoid being set onto Boue St Michel, until well clear of the Passage, when Godin bears 255°.

On this transit Tautenay and Platte Fougère appear over the south head (drying 6·1m) of Petite Longue Pierre (height 2m). This head must not be confused with the SW head (drying 5·8m).

The sketch of the transit in the late Malcolm Robson's pilot shows Tautenay and Platte Fougère over the SW head and this has been copied into another transit book. In good visibility there will be no confusion as Platte Fougère will appear too far to the south on this line. However, even after several visits, the haze was such that the editor was unable to obtain a clear picture of Platte Fougère, and in these conditions the error of aligning Tautenay with the SW head will lead straight on to Boue St Michel!

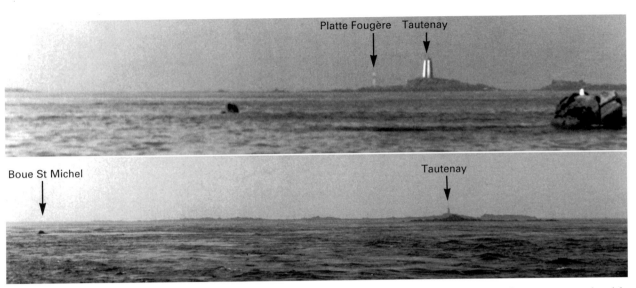

Photo H27B

Photo H27B shows the correct transit (before low water), above the incorrect transit with Boue St Michel showing far left.

Second option

Below half tide the SW head (drying 5·8m) and the S head (drying 6·1m) of Petite Longue Pierre will be above water as will Demie (drying 5·8m), known locally as Demie Carré, so called as it is a half tide rock, situated at the east end of the passage. These rocks are set in a curve and are steep-to.

From Transit H25 112°, identify Longue Pierre (height 13m) and Grande Amfroque (height 17m) with its two beacon towers, 1M NE of Longue Pierre. When Grande Amfroque closes on Longue Pierre take:

Transit H28 055° – Grande Amfroque beacon to the left of Longue Pierre.

When 300m off the SW head, turn to starboard and follow the curve formed by the SW head, the S head and Demie at 200m distance until Tautenay is over the S head (Transit H27A 296°), which may appear near half tide as a cluster of small heads. Then steer out with the stern transit H27 296° until Godin bears 255°.

ROUND THE ISLAND (Grade EC)

Should the intention be to spend some time at Herm and explore the anchorages it would be advisable first to make a tour of the island on foot at low water.

South of Herm the water is deep, but to the north and west there are some three square miles of sand, with rocky outcrops, which are more or less dry at LW. While the soundings for the rocks on Admiralty *808* may be relied upon, some of the channels are silting and the depths over sand are less than those shown on the chart.

Starting from the anchorage between Mouette and the Rosière Steps, steer south until clear of Meulettes (see Transit H19) and, when Transit H20 047° shows that you are clear to turn to port, come round, leaving Moulinet (Boue au Port, height 1m) 50m to port, steer to pass inside Selle Roque (Saddle Rock), noting that it extends north some 150m and drying rocks stretch out 100m from the point of Herm opposite.

There is a pleasant anchorage, out of the tide and protected from winds from the west in Putrainez Bay south of Putrainez (height 9m).

To clear outside Putrainez use as a stern transit:

Transit H29 227° – Grande Fauconnière open of the SE cliff of Herm.

BELVOIR BAY

Leaving Caquorobert (height 15m) 200m to port you can anchor in Belvoir Bay. Anchor on a line between Moulière and Caquorobert where there will be some protection from the stream which runs on either side of this line. On small neaps it is possible to anchor with caution, on soundings closer inshore. Recently a yacht aground in the bay was lost due to being overwhelmed by waves which arose with the rising tide.

SHELL BAY

This shallow anchorage is popular with locals for a picnic and swim and can be used with care by visitors. The north side of Moulière (height 2m) is clean, and entry, avoiding rocks to the north of the anchorage, can be made on 271°, a line between Noire Pute and the café on the beach (see plan). Anchor on soundings on sand but avoid taking the ground.

Continuing round the island

Alternatively, continuing round Herm, the stern transit H29 will take you northeast, clear of Aiguillons (drying 3m) and the outliers southeast of Equitelais (drying 2·9m).

When Godin bears 310° or Grande Amfroque 005°, steer north and come round into Le Boursée Passage east to west (Transit H27 back to H24) with due regard to the stream and to Boue St Michel.

Horse Rock (drying 1·5m) and Cavale (drying 1·2m) are outliers to the reefs NW of Herm, so do not leave Transit H24 until Belvedere House is in transit with the white patch on Castle Cornet 223° (Transit G05 page 30).

Passing Roustel and before taking the Corbette or Rocquerie Passage to return to the Rosière Steps, an anchorage may be found northwest of Herm by passing between Cavale and Rousse, using as a stern transit:

Transit H30 269° – Platte light beacon under the south face of Vale Castel. Note from the photo that the new concrete chimney and the old northern chimney of the power station are in line on this bearing. The two old steel chimneys may be dismantled at some future date but the concrete chimney may be used for Transit H26 (page 66).

Enter on transit H30 and follow it to anchor, out of the strong tidal flow, on soundings in a sandy patch between the rocks NW of Pierre aux Rats obelisk.

ROCQUERIE PASSAGE AND ANCHORAGE (Grade M)

The Rocquerie Passage (depth 4m or more to 300m NW of Vermerette Bn) is 200m wide and can be taken by steering 146° on a course parallel to the line joining Fondu (8m) and

Rocquerie (5m), leaving them about 120m to port. The stern transit on this course, leading into the Percée Passage is:

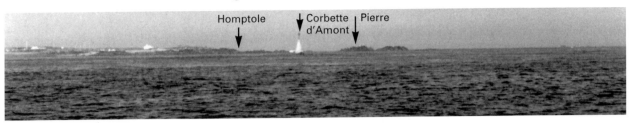

Transit H31 326° – Corbette d'Amont lying between Homptole and Pierre off Beaucette Marina.

For the Rocquerie anchorage which can be used at low water, starting at the junction of the Alligande, Creux and Corbette passages, steer into the Rocquerie Passage with the stern transit:

Transit H32 164° – House on Jethou over Epec Bn.

200m south of Rocquerie steer to starboard and anchor in 2m sand 100m east of the rock.

ANOTHER PASSAGE AND ANCHORAGE

The passage and anchorage described below are popular with local yachtsmen. Accidents occur even to the experienced and visitors should not use them without a local as pilot on board.

LE DUIT DE CHERCREUX (Grade H)

(Depths uncertain. A 'duit' is a fast flowing stream)

The Shell Bay anchorage is shallow and south of Chercreux the channel is silting. The editor has been through Le Duit with an experienced local yachtsman, against a 3–4 knot tide (to enable us to stop!). It is usual to make an inspection at low water before attempting this passage.

The plan, page 57, shows Shell Bay. The depths given on Admiralty *808* are unreliable and the positions of the rocks on either side of the channel are best observed at low water. Admiralty *262a* gives a better picture than *808*.

No track is sketched on the plan. After passing La Pointe du Gentilhomme, Transit H33 enabled the editor and his local friend to clear into deep water.

Proceed up the middle of the 'ditch', against the tide, leaving Chercreux (drying 8·2m) to starboard and other rocks, some drying nearly 8m, to port and to starboard. This is an area where silting has occurred and depths are much reduced. Identify the marks for the stern transits:

Transits H33 175° to 172° (Track not shown on the plan)

First bring the conspicuous tree over the lower, left-hand rock on 175° and gradually move it until it is over the higher right-hand rock on 172°.

When Tautenay is about 0·4M off on the starboard bow, turn to port and take Transit H24 (page 65) into the Little Russel.

THE HUMPS (Grade H)

There is a popular low-water anchorage in the Humps when the rocks and sands between Canuette, Galeu, Peak and Godin are dry. For first entry a bow lookout to spot the isolated submerged rocks and an experienced local yachtsman on board as pilot are essentials.

Note The Guernsey Board of Administration requests that boat owners do not land on the Humps between the 1st January and 15th of July to protect the important breeding sea bird colonies on these islets. The same applies to Brehon Tower. Several vessels visited the tower in the spring of 1994 and the tern population failed to breed.

COMING FROM BELVOIR BAY

Transit H34 028° – Grande Amfroque over the exposed end of Les Fosses will pass between Sardinias (height 2m) and Aiguillons (drying 3m) to the entrance of the Usurie Passage.

Gde Amfroque

Photo H35 Entering the Humps anchorage from the SE at LW. Canuette is on the left of the picture.

Turn into the stream, keeping in the northern half of the passage as there are several below-water rocks in the southern half. Follow the curve of the outlying rocks showing off Les Fosses and, with a careful lookout over the bow to avoid the spur of rocks shown on the plan, round up into the anchorage on sand in 1m LAT.

It is essential to leave before the beach covers on the flood as, once covered, the stream rips through the anchorage making a dinghy return to the yacht and departure dangerous.

After visiting the Humps anchorage at LW neaps, his 'pilot' took the editor through the channels to the west and southwest. The rocks on either side were clearly visible and the recent silting was evident off the S and SE end of Chercreux as La Pointe du Gentilhomme was approached.

Marks around Herm and Guernsey

Grande Amfroque from south

Roustel from SE

Vale Mill from the east

Noire Pute

Platte Beacon with Vale Mill to the left

Rousse

Tautenay

Sark

Creux Harbour 49°25'·85N 2°20'·5W
Maseline Harbour 49°26'·05N 2°20'·5W
Dixcart Bay 49°25'·4N 2°20'·4W
Havre Gosselin 49°25'·8N 2°22'·5W

Sark Mill and St Peter's church have long been shown on charts as marks but they are no longer conspicuous and alternatives have to be found.

The absence of motorcars and marinas is a major contribution to the peace of this beautiful island.

During the 14th and 15th centuries Sark was so frequently raided by pirates that the only inhabitants were a few hermits, living in the ruins of abandoned monasteries.

In 1565 Queen Elizabeth granted 'the Island of Sark in our Dutchy of Normandy' to Helier de Carteret, Seigneur of St Ouen, Jersey. The condition was that, within two years, he was to see that the island was continually inhabited, with not less than forty men each armed with a musket and capable of its defence. Two cannon were also provided for this purpose.

De Carteret occupied the island with 39 families and their retainers, most from Jersey but some, with the help of his friend Nicholas Gosselin, from Guernsey. He divided the island into 40 *ténéments* of which 39 were leased in perpetuity to his followers as feudal holdings. The present day system of government of the island evolved from the feudal constitution that his followers had sworn to uphold.

A company was floated in 1838 to exploit the silver deposits discovered on Little Sark above Port Gorey. A deep shaft was sunk and a rich vein discovered. According to the story, samples for assessing were entrusted to the captain of a St Sampson cutter for conveyance to England.

On hearing that his wife was sick, he first made for St Sampson but his ship struck on the Brayes and was lost with all hands. On the same day Father Neptune invaded the shaft. The pumps were incapable of ejecting him and the project was abandoned. The mine chimneys remain as an aid to entry to Port Gorey (see page 84).

Contact with the outside world is maintained by means of ferries from St Peter Port and, while there is a primary school on the island, children must cross to Guernsey for their secondary education.

Brecqhou is privately owned and landing is not permitted. The profile of the island has recently been altered by the construction of a large building.

Charts

Admiralty *808*, *3654* or, if obtainable, *262A*. Admiralty *808* and *3654* are based on European Datum.

Lights

1. **Point Robert** 49°26'·2N 2°20'·7W Fl.15s65m20M Horn(2)30s 138°-vis-353° White 8-sided tower

2. **Bec du Nez** 49°27'·1N 2°22'·1W Fl(4)WR.15s14m8M 057°-W-230°-R-057° White wood structure 1m
3. **Basse Blanchard** 49°25'·4N 2°17'·3W E card buoy Q(3)10s Bell

Yachts should not approach Sark at night but, with due consideration to weather and tide, several delightful anchorages may be discovered by day.

The plateau is mostly between 75 and 100 metres high and, from 2M off on first approach, the cliffs appear disconcertingly featureless.

When planning a visit, as with all the Channel Islands, it is essential to make good use of the tides and to consider the weather conditions.

The shape of the island and its position in the main tidal stream accelerates the flow which at the top of a big spring tide can reach 7 knots in the Gouliot between Brecqhou and Sark. Outside the two harbours, the stream in the Goulet reaches 6 knots on the ebb.

Coming from Guernsey and making for Creux or Maseline on the east coast, the decision whether to go north or south depends on the state of the tide. At half tide down and half tide up the stream is generally slack all round the island.

Offshore, the northeast stream is strongest at high water and the southwest stream at low water. It follows that, from the Bec du Nez in the north to the Grande Moie it is slack at high water, and from Sercul to Grande Grève it is slack at low water.

Go north therefore, coming from the west at high water and southabout at low water when there will be about nine hours of NE stream between L'Etac and Creux harbour.

Leaving the east coast of Sark and bound north-about for St Peter Port, make use of the eddy in Banquette Bay which runs from an hour before high water to half tide down while the stream in the Big Russel is running NE (see page 136).

Tidal levels referred to chart datum
La Maseline Jetty 49°26'·05N 2°20'·5W
MHWS 9·0m MHWN 6·6m MLWN 3·5m MLWS 1·0m

Sark tidal streams

The editor is most grateful to Mr R. Adams for providing the information on the tidal streams around Sark and for the tide chart on page 136.

Miss Bell, chairwoman of the Sark Pilotage Committee and Mr Adams also kindly provided some of the transit photographs.

The tides around Sark vary all round the coast. At the Point du Nez (Bec du Nez on Admiralty *808*) the tidal flow starts running to the west a little before high water, even up to an hour before high water on a big spring tide, and runs toward Brecqhou, curving to the west as it approaches the current coming north through the Gouliot Passage; the streams meet between La Givaude and Brecqhou, the tidal flow then running northeast, while inshore, along the coast of Sark, the stream runs in the opposite direction.

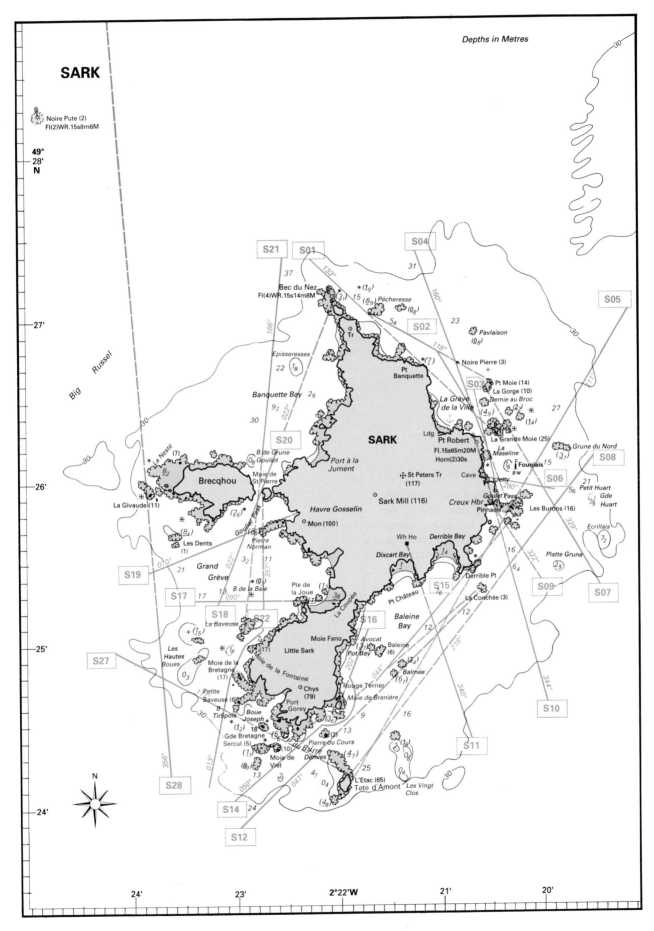

SARK

Noire Pute (2)
Fl(2)WR.15s8m6M

49°
28'
N

27'

Big Russel

26'

25'

24'

Depths in Metres

S21 S01

S04

S05

37   133°   31

Bec du Nez
Fl(4)WR.15s14m8M

*(1₉)
(3₁) 15 (8₉) Pécheresse
54   (0₈)

S02

160°

Episseresses
22 (1₈)

186°

Banquette Bay 2₆

9₂ 022°

30

S20

B de Grune
(0₈) Gouliot
Moie de
St Pierre

La Nesté (7)
(8₂)

Brecqhou

La Givaude (11)

(2₆)*

(8₄)
Les Dents
(1)

070° 21

Grand
Grève

S19

S17 17 1₃

S18

S22

La Baveuse

Les
Hautes
Boues

(0₃)

S27

Petite
Baveuse (6)
B
Tiriphols
(1₂) 18
Boue
Joseph
Gde Bretagne (6₆)
Sercul (5)
(1₁)
(8₉) 13

Moie de
Viet

S28

N

S14 24

S12

*(7)
Noire Pierre (3)
+

Pavlaison
(0₈)

23

Pt
Banquette

118°

La Grève
de la Ville

SARK

St Peters Tr
(117)

Sark Mill (116)

Port à la
Jument

Havre Gosselin

Mon (100)

Pierre
Norman

3₂ 11
357°

(0₄)
*(1₃)

B de la Baie

Pte de
la Joue

090°

La Coupée

Moie Fano

Little Sark

Moie de la Fontaine

Chys
(79)

Port
Gorey

Pot
Boue

Gde Bretagne
(6₆)

Pierre du Cours
(2)

Moie de
Demies

013° 050° 047°

4₇

Wh Ho

Dixcart Bay

(1₄)

Derrible Bay

1₄

1

S15

Pt Château

Ldg Pt Robert
Fl.15s65m20M
Horn(2)30s

Cave

Derrible Pt

16

6₄

S09

La Maseline

Creux Hbr

Pinnacle

Goulet Pass

Pt Moie (14)
La Gorge (10)
Demie au Broc
(2₃)
(4₉) *
(1₄)

La Grande Moie (25)

Foumais 15
6
B W

280° Jetty

322° 329°

Platte Grune
(2₉)

(8₄) 2₉

S06

S08

21 Petit Huart
56   Gde
Huart

Ecrillais
(7₂)

S07

12

S10

Baleine
Bay

12

Avocat
Baleine
(6)

Balmée
(6₇)

(2₄)

(4₅)
Rouge Terrier
Moie de Brenière

9 16

218°

La Conchée (3)

(1₉)
(2) (0₈)
(0₈)
(0₄)

Rue Pierre Cours Demies
(4₇)

25

L'Etac (65)
Tete d'Amont

Les Vingt
Clos

30

Grune du Nord
(3₇)

27

S03

S11

30

73

In the Gouliot Passage the stream runs at about the same time as in the Big Russel, but immediately north of Gouliot it starts running north before low water and runs right up to the Point du Nez where it meets the southwest stream running down the Big Russel. It continues to do so until nearly high water. It runs with great force from half flood until an hour before high water.

At the Pécheresse, east of Point du Nez, the stream starts running southeast at high water and runs in that direction until half ebb when it runs northwest until low water. It then runs southeast until two hours before high water, then runs to the northwest until high water, when it runs to the southeast again.

Note that the southeast tidal flow starts at the Pécheresse, or just to the north of it, and runs along the coast as far as the Founiais, then turns with the northeast tides of the Big Russel out past the Grande Moie to a line where the Conchée just shows inside the Burons.

Nearly 1M outside Pavilaison it turns, running more northerly; it runs more northerly the further north it goes until it joins the stream going north up the Big Russel.

There is a weaker counter-eddy inside Grève de la Ville.

In the Goulet Passage the stream runs about the same as in the Big Russel, but is always a little earlier in changing to ebb or to flow.

At the Conchée the southwest stream starts running at half ebb and continues running until about low water, or just before, depending upon the type of spring tide, whilst at the Pierre du Cours it runs southwest from half ebb until nearly one hour after low water, when it changes and runs in an easterly direction until half ebb.

Inshore, taking a line from Brenière to Baleine and Derrible Bay, the stream runs in a southwesterly direction from high water until about low water, but not with any great force, except at the headlands.

The stream in the Vingt Clos and east of L'Etac runs at about the same as the Pierre du Cours.

At Sercul the stream starts running southeast at low water, reaching great strength at half flood, whilst ½M west of Sercul it starts running in a northerly direction towards the Hautes Boues and Brecqhou. However, on a big spring tide, the westerly flow turns to the south, one hour after half flood and runs powerfully for 1½–2 hours, or nearly to high water. The stream then turns to the north until half ebb, when it turns to the southwest until low water.

The southwesterly flow is not strong until the Bec du Nez is open with La Nesté (a rock drying 8·2m north of La Givaude), as it is in the lee of the islands, particularly of Brecqhou.

MASELINE HARBOUR FROM THE NORTH (Grade EC)

Bec du Nez, at the northern tip of Sark, is steep-to but there are overfalls northwest of the rock with wind against tide.

The channel described below is narrow (100m wide in one place) and should not be attempted at low water springs.

Coming from Guernsey or the Big Russel the passage is best taken at HW when the stream will be slack between Bec du Nez and the Grande Moie.

Photo S01B

Photo S01A

Transit S01 133° – The right-hand side of Grande Moie x Banquette Point. Photo S01A is a distant view from the north of Bec du Nez. Photo S01B, taken near LW neaps shows the Pécheresse rocks (drying 8·9m), foreground left, with Petite Moie and La Gorge behind. A rock drying 7m off Pt Banquette, is showing in front of Grande Moie.

South of Pécheresse is a point with a spur drying 6·6m forming the NW arm of Les Fontaines Bay with a reef running out 200m and drying 4·5m, 400m to the east.

With Pécheresse abeam, identify the black, above-water rock Noire Pierre (height 3m) and alter to port for:

Transit S02 118° – The north face of Noire Pierre ✗ the north face of Petite Moie.

When 200m off Noire Pierre, steer for the gap between Pt Robert (with the lighthouse) and Grande Moie. The dangers under the lighthouse are cleared by:

Transit S03 165° – Pinnacle Rock of the Goulet just open of the end of the Maseline Jetty.

Note that Pinnacle Rock is misplaced on Admiralty *808* and should be further east.

Anchorage

Anchor anywhere NW of the jetty, but at least 50m clear to allow for the movement of the ferries. Coming alongside briefly is possible, with a least depth of 4m but it is strictly reserved for commercial vessels.

With reference to Admiralty *808* or, if available, *262A* there is an anchorage, away from traffic and swell, in La Grève de la Ville to the NW of Pt Robert. Close in to some stone steps it is shingle and sand in 7m. A cliff path leads quite close to a pub which serves meals, and shops are nearby.

(Grade M)

A more open approach, particularly when sailing, which avoids the overfalls off Bec du Nez, is to steer east, leaving the Bec ½M to starboard, with St Martin's Pt (Guernsey) open to the right of Bec du Nez and when:

Transit S04 160° – all Les Burons are open of Pt Robert on 160° (photo Sark Pilotage), steer down on this transit but leave Noire Pierre to port, to Maseline. Pass west of Noire Pierre as, when passing east you will get too close to Demie au Broc (drying 4·9m).

In the photo the easterly part of Les Burons is hidden behind Noire Pierre.

MASELINE FROM THE NORTHEAST (Grade M)

Founiais, drying 6·7m and marked by a beacon with an 'F' topmark, lies 300m ENE of Maseline pierhead with Grune du Nord drying 3·7m 900m from the pierhead on the same line. The stream runs strongly over Grune du Nord when it is covered and there are eddies to the south.

The approach, when coming from the Alderney Race, will leave Grune du Nord 100m to port:

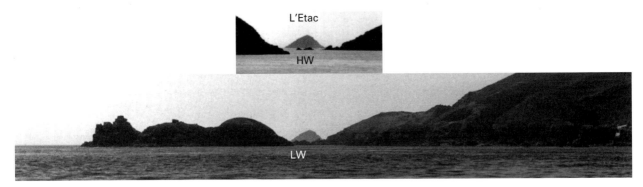

Transit S05 211° – L'Etac between Les Burons and Sark.

This approach can be used for either Maseline or Creux Harbour, passing north of Grune du Nord (drying 3·7m) but Transit S08 (see below) may be preferred as an approach from the northeast if La Conchée can be identified from a distance.

For Maseline, with care, pass either side 100m from Founiais beacon.

LEAVING MASELINE HARBOUR (Grade M)

Low in the cliff, opposite to the pierhead, is a round cave mouth. To leave the harbour passing south of Founiais:

Transit S06 280° – Cave just open of the pierhead as a stern transit.

TO CLEAR SARK TO THE SOUTHEAST TAKE AS A STERN TRANSIT

Transit S07 329° – The remarkable La Gorge with its 'head' looking west, open to the right of La Grande Moie by a distance equal to the distance between the two peaks of La Grande Moie.

Photo S07

Note in the photo Pt Robert LtHo far left with Founiais Bn left centre.

This course will leave Ecrillais rocks (depth 7·2m) to port and Platte Grune with only 2·9m over it to starboard, or proceed to:

CREUX HARBOUR FROM THE NORTH OR NORTHEAST (Grade M)

From the north, it is forbidden to pass south through the drying Goulet Passage between Creux and Les Burons and so, after passing between Pt Robert and Grande Moie, steer out to port to take Transit S07 as a stern transit, identify La Conchée and take:

Transit S08 218° – L'Etac well open to the left of La Conchée. (Photo Sark Pilotage)

Proceeding on this course Creux Harbour wall will open from behind Les Burons and the approach is clear between drying rocks when:

Transit S09 322° – the beach at the back of the harbour fills the entrance.

From the northeast, an approach can be made using Transit S08 218° (above) and, avoiding the dogleg of S05–S07 proceeding until the beach fills the entrance.

However, overfalls may be encountered between Grune du Nord (drying 3·7m) and Petit Huart (5·6m below datum so not dangerous), and care should be taken to avoid being set onto the Grune.

Note that the striking mark for Boue Grune du Nord, with 1·5m over it situated 200m SE of Grune du Nord, is with La Conchée on the middle of L'Etac.

If unable to identify La Conchée from a distance, approach on Transit S05 211° (above) and, leaving Grune du Nord to port, take Transit S07 329° (above) as a stern transit, followed by S08 218° and S09 320°.

CREUX HARBOUR FROM THE SOUTHEAST (Grade M)

Point Robert lighthouse, painted white, is visible from a distance. The entrance to the harbour is clear when:

Transit S10 344° – Pt Robert lighthouse x Creux Harbour tunnel.

As an alternative, Mr Adams prefers to see the Grand Moie in the middle of the Goulet, i.e. between the Burons and the land.

Creux Harbour dries. Anchorage may be found outside with reference to the chart. By arrangement it might be possible to borrow a mooring or to lean against the wall inside the harbour.

Facilities

Passing through the Creux or Maseline tunnels, a track leads up to the village where there is a bank (open Mon–Fri 1000–1230 and 1400–1500) post office and other shops. Distributed across the island are several pubs, hotels and restaurants. Visitors may walk, hire bicycles or take a ride in a horse-drawn carriage.

It may be possible to obtain petrol and diesel from the power station or from Mr Colin Guille who provides transport to the top of the hill.

Note

As a stern transit, Transit S08, passing between Grune du Nord and Petit and Grand Huart, is useful when leaving Sark to the north for Alderney or the Race.

DIXCART AND DERRIBLE BAYS (Grade M)

These two bays, side by side on the SE coast of Sark, are popular anchorages for visiting yachts. They are sheltered from winds except from the SE quarter but a southwesterly swell can come up round L'Etac and disturb rest at night.

From the northeast

Approaching La Conchée on Transit S08 218°, pass it on either side at a distance of at least 100m to clear the drying extent of the rock, and either bay may then be entered, leaving Pt Chateau and/or Derrible Pt 200m to starboard.

Anchor on sand as close to the beach as soundings, tide and other yachts permit.

Paths lead up from both beaches, the more gentle gradient being that from Dixcart Bay.

Dixcart from the southeast

Sark Mill is no longer conspicuous and disappears when 1M from the bay on the 337° transit shown on Admiralty *808*. The transit now used by the pilots is:

Transit S11 340° – The white house over the westward slope of Point Chateau. In 1994 Mr Adams reported that 'the white house' was due for repainting and may finish another colour. If so it is hoped that it will remain as conspicuous as in the photo!

SOUTHABOUT TO THE EAST COAST ANCHORAGES

An approach southabout is best made at low water when, from one hour after low water, the stream will run northeast for nearly nine hours from Sercul rock, south of Little Sark, to Creux Harbour.

A glance at chart *808* will show the shallows and disturbed water southeast of Little Sark and care must be taken not to be swept onto Les Vingt Clos or Balmée, both of which cover, when the stream is running.

For a first time approach, pass ½M south of L'Etac and then steer 060° to reach Transit S11 340° for Dixcart Bay, S10 344° for Creux or, using S08, S07 and S06 as necessary for Maseline.

PASSAGES INSIDE L'ETAC (Grade EC)

These passages need not be considered severe after familiarisation with the island and when the outlying named rocks have been identified for future recognition.

The dangers when passing from the west are:
1. Rocks drying 8·9m 300m south of Sercul (height 5m).
2. A rock covered by 2m at LWS 400m ESE of '1' above.)
3. Demies, the reef drying 4·7m running out 400m NNW of L'Etac.
4. The drying rocks extending 100m W to NW of Pierre du Cours (height 2m).
5. Drying rocks extending up to 300m out from the SE coast of Little Sark.
6. Rocks drying 3·6m extending up to 100m south of Moie de Brenière.

From a position 0·75M off the southern point of Little Sark bearing 030°, make a positive identification of Pierre du Cours (height 2m) with La Conchée (height 3m) 2M distant SE of Derrible Point and take:

Transit S12 047° –La Conchée well open to the right of Pierre du Cours and Balmée (if above water) visible between them.

The photo shows Balmée too close to Pierre du Cours and this transit would pass very close south of the 2m rock.

When 200m from Pierre du Cours alter to leave it 80m to port and then steer out to leave Balmée to port or take the inshore passage below.

An alternative, which may be preferred, to clear north of Pierre du Cours, is to come in with:

Transit S14 050° – La Conchée and Balmée open to the right of Moie de Brenière to pass north of the 2m rock.

The photo, taken at LW shows the high-water line on Moie de Brenière and the drying rocks off the point. When taking this passage at high water, Balmée will be covered and La Conchée should appear well open of the point to obtain the same transit and avoid close approach to danger '5' (see above).

When taking this passage, on approaching Pierre du Cours, the rock must be cleared by more than 100m to avoid danger '4', and, when the rock bears south, steer east to avoid the rocks south of Moie de Brenière, danger '6'.

At LW come further north with Balmée open of Brenière Point on 052° (Conchée may be obscured behind the point).

INSHORE PASSAGE (Grade EC)

From Transit S14, When Pierre du Cours bears south, steer east to clear the rocks (danger '6') showing in the photo which was taken at LW.

When clear of these rocks, come round to the north, leaving Moie de Brenière 200m to port.

Rouge Terrier, a small bay north of Brenière provides a protected anchorage with a landing and cliff path to the plateau.

The next bay to the north, Pot Bay, is also an anchorage but, if these are not to be visited, passage north to Dixcart Bay may be made inside Balmée (drying 6·7m) and Demie de Balmée with:

Transit S15 044° – Les Burons Chimney in the 'V' of Derrible Point. Do not pass too close to Balmée as a shelf extends a short distance to the west, or too close to Baleine as heads dry 100m to the south.

Passage north inside Baleine (height 6m) and Avocat (drying 3·7m) may be made with the stern transit:

Transit S16 202° – Daylight just showing through the hole in Brenière. Beware of Avocat which may be covered and rocks drying 5m extending 100m east from Moie Fano.

West coast anchorages

LA GRANDE GREVE

Entry from the west (Grade M)

The southern entry passes between La Baveuse (drying 7·6m), with Les Hautes Boues, drying 1·5m and more, extending 0·4M to the west, and Boue de la Baie, awash at LW, to the north of the line. Take:

Transit S17 090° – Right-hand end of La Coupée x Pointe de la Joue.

When 400m from Pointe de la Joue turn to port and come to anchor 400m NE of the point on fine sand and shingle in 7m.

HAVRE GOSSELIN (Grade M)

If approaching on Transit S17, to clear west of Boue de la Baie, turn north when:

Transit S18 022° – Bec du Nez just seen through the Gouliot Passage.

Yhe transit Sark Mill and monument in line 070° shown on Admiralty *808* cannot be used for a direct approach to Havre Gosselin as the mill is invisible. An alternative transit which will leave Les Dents (height 1m) south of Brecqhou 200m to port, makes use of the conspicuous Fissure on the north side well into the Havre.

Transit S19 070° – Gosselin Fissure over or to the left of Pierre Norman (drying 8·8m).

When Bec du Nez is seen through the Gouliot (Transit S18), turn to port and come round into the anchorage, anchoring in 8m clear of other yachts.

Havre Gosselin makes a snug anchorage exposed only to the SW but rest at night may be disturbed by a rolling swell that can build up in the harbour at certain states of the tide.

There is a good dinghy landing, with steps, an iron ladder, and 299 steps up the cliff lead to a pub.

If leaving Havre Gosselin on the reciprocal of S18, turn west before crossing S17 to avoid Les Hautes Boues.

THE GOULIOT PASSAGE (Grade M)

The passage is clean on both sides, with a least depth of 2·6m. There is a boue (drying 1·2m) 100m SW of Moie St Pierre, one (drying 2·6m) 200m SW of the Brecqhou side and Boue de Grune Gouliot, with 0·8m over it, 600m NNW of the passage.

Tide tables should be consulted before making the passage. At the top of springs the northerly stream can reach 7 knots. Slack water is at half tide.

Photo S20

Passage north S20 022°

Ensure that Bec du Nez is well open of Moie St Pierre and do not turn west for Herm until well past Boue de Grune Gouliot or, continuing north keep clear to the west of Petite Banquette (depth 4·2m) and Episseresses (depth 1·8m) by holding as a stern transit:

Moie St Pierre   Moie de la Bretagne

S21 186° – Moie de la Bretagne open of Moie St Pierre.

Passage south

Transit S21 186° should be followed into the passage, clearing Episseresses and Petite Banquette.

The photo shows the crane in use in the construction of the 'mediaeval castle' on Brecqhou in 1994.

Note the anchorage in Port à la Jument NE of Moie St Pierre (see plan).

INSHORE PASSAGES SOUTHABOUT FROM THE EAST COAST TO HAVRE GOSSELIN

The passage south of Sercul and then inside La Baveuse is difficult and the passage inside Moie de Viet and Grande Bretagne should certainly not be undertaken unless someone already familiar with the passage is on board. Boue Joseph has even caught several of the experts and, probably for safety, the area is shown on Admiralty *808* as drying although it carries 4m at LWS.

The rocks in this area are so crowded that pilotage is by rock recognition rather than by transits and the photographs below are an aid to recognition.

FROM DIXCART BAY AND SOUTH OF SERCUL (Grade EC)

Time the passage to arrive south of Sercul at LW when the stream is slack, using the directions for the inshore passage on pages 78 and 79 in reverse starting with Transit S16,

The Pierre du Burre Passage at LW

Havre de Gosselin

then rounding Moie de Brenière and taking Transit S14 or S12, passing 500m south of Sercul.

A slow turn may then be made to the NW and when the peak of Moie de St Pierre (at the Gouliot) bears 013° and it is open its width of Moie de la Bretagne (no photo) steer on this transit with care, leaving Boue Tirlipois (drying 1·1m) at least 100m to starboard.

When Petite Baveuse (height 6m), which extends westward at LW, is abeam to starboard 200m off, steer to leave Moie de la Bretagne (height 17m) 200m to starboard. Then come round to starboard, steering to leave Moie de la Fontaine (height 17m) 100m to starboard.

Then, keeping 200m off the coast and leaving La Baveuse (drying 7·6m) 200m to port, proceed until:

Transit S22 357° – Pierre Norman (drying 8·8m) is in transit with the Gouliot.

Then steer on this transit, leaving the dangers of Boue de la Baie (drying 0·3m) to port.

Note that in the photograph, taken near HW neaps, only the top of Pierre Norman is showing.

When 200m from Pierre Norman steer to port and, rounding the rock at a distance of 200m, enter Havre Gosselin.

Photo S23

PORT GOREY

If a visit to Port Gorey is intended, the bay will open when Sercul is abaft the beam steering on the 013° transit and one or more of the chimneys of the abandoned silver mine will be seen (Photo S23.)

Turning to starboard steer 050° for the middle of the bay, with the most conspicuous chimney seen fine to starboard. Grande Bretagne (18m) must be left 100m to starboard, as the entry between rocks drying 7·8m on the north side and 2·2m on the south is only 100m wide (see plan page 73) as is the cove itself.

Anchor in 3m according to tide. The bottom is rocky but a patch of sand may be found.

Transit S27 (page 86) may be used when leaving Port Gorey and will lead out north of Tirlipois and clear to the NW, south of Les Hautes Boues. To clear to the west, follow the course of 230° as described under Transit S27 and steer west when clear of Tirlipois.

THE PIERRE DU BURRE PASSAGE (PAST BOUE JOSEPH) (Grade H)

Do not attempt this passage without a local expert on board.

See photo S24, taken from position 'x' on the plan. It shows, looking north of west at 1½hr before LWN, arrowed from left to right:

Photo S24

A. Sercul with the drying 8·9m rock to the left of it.
B. Moie de Viet.
C. Grande Bretagne.
D. Petite Baveuse.
E. Little Sark. At this state of tide, the Pierre du Burre is just appearing between Grande Bretagne and Petite Baveuse.

After passing north of Pierre du Cours with the stern transit S14 050°, turn to starboard to pass between Moie de Viet (height 10m) and the Pierre du Burre (drying 6·6m)

Photo S25

See Photo S25, taken at LW. Admiralty *808* shows the whole area as drying (for safety?) but there is 4m in the channel and Admiralty *262A* gives a better picture.

Now to avoid Boue Joseph!

Photo S26

Photo S26, taken looking SE at LWS, shows the gap between Pierre du Burre on the left and Moie de Viet on the right. Boue Joseph with a seagull to the right of it is arrowed.

When Pierre du Burre is abeam to starboard steer to starboard to pass 50m off the above-water rock close to Little Sark (shown on the plan). You may then enter Port Gorey or, to pass out to the NW between Boue Tirlipois (drying 1·1m) and the rock drying 1·2m 100m SSW of Petite Baveuse (6m) take:

Transit S27 117° – Tête d'Amont a rock close to the NE side of L'Etac in the 'V' formed by the NE side of Moie de Viet and the SW side of Grande Bretagne.

When well clear of Boue Tirlipois come round when you see the Gouliot Passage to the north steering to leave Moie de la Bretagne 100m to starboard and passing between Moie de la Fontaine (height 17m) and La Baveuse (drying 7·6m) as with the previous track.

As an alternative, passing south of Boue Tirlipois, steer out on 230° with the middle of Port Gorey cove bearing 050°, leaving Grande Bretagne 100m to port and coming round to the north when clear west of Boue Tirlipois, to pass inshore of La Baveuse as above.

Transit S27 117°

LEAVING SARK FOR GUERNSEY BY THE SOUTH

All dangers on the west of Sark are cleared when:

Transit S28 356° – Grande Amfroque (height 17m) is open to the west of La Givaude (height 11m).

Grande Amfroque is 6M to the north and may be invisible in haze or over the horizon for a small yacht, in which case it is sufficient to ensure that La Givaude, off the western end of Brecqhou, bears due north.

Jersey

Jersey is the largest, most commercial, most populated of all the islands, with, in season, a larger influx of visitors and holidaymakers than the rest of the islands put together. But also you will find friendly people and beautiful country, with uncrowded anchorages and miniature harbours around the coast.

St Helier harbour has now been extended, with a RoRo terminal and two marinas with a third under construction. The harbour staff are most helpful to visiting yachtsmen. However, being closer to France, you will encounter more ferries and commercial traffic than when entering or leaving St Peter Port, and in summer the town is more crowded with visitors coming from Granville and St Malo.

Since you may only enter Jersey at St Helier or Gorey, the main approaches given here aim for these harbours.

Fortunately Jersey coasts are well lit and marked by first class beacons which are maintained by the States of Jersey Harbours and Airport Committee who are responsible for all the navigational aids.

Charts

Admiralty *2669, 3665, 1136, 1137, 1138*. European Datum. Photocopies of the older charts *3667, 62a, 62b,* and *62c* may be obtainable from the Hydrographic Office.
Imray *C33A*, and *C33B* (southern approaches)

Note The magnetic variation 2M south of St Helier is 4°20'W 1995, decreasing 7·2' annually. The compass rose on Admiralty *1137* is incorrect.

Lights for approaches to St Helier

1. **Grosnez Point** 49°15'·5N 2°14'·7W
   Fl(2)WR.15s50m19/17M 081°-W-188°-R-241°
   White hut
2. **La Corbière** 49°10'·8N 2°14'·9W
   Iso.WR.10s36m18/16M Stone tower Shore-W-294°-R-328°-W-148°-R-shore. Horn Mo(C)60s RC *CB* (-·-/·-··) 295·5kHz 20M Synchronised with horn for distance off. Wind speed and direction: Signal *CB* 3 times (16s) long dash 8s, a series of 1–8 short dashes for wind direction in eight cardinal points: 1=NE, 2=E, ... to 8=N, a series of 1–8 pips for average wind speed: 1=force 1 ... 8=force 8 Beaufort, one or more short dashes to indicate strength of gusts above average wind speed.
3. **Noirmont Point** 49°10'·0N 2°10'·0W
   Fl(4)12s18m13M Black tower, white bands.
4. **Demie de Pas** 49°09'·1N 2°06'·0W
   Mo(D)WR.12s11m14/10M Horn(3)60s 303°-W-130°-R-303° Black tower yellow top Racon
5. **Platte Rock** 49°10'·2N 2°07'·3W Fl.R.1·5s6m5M
   Red column
6. **Western Passage Ldg Lts 082°**
   La Grève d'Azette 49°10'·2N 2°05'·0W
   Front Oc.5s23m14M 034°-vis-129° White column, red rectangle

   Rear Mont Ubé 1M to rear Oc.R.5s46m12M 250°-vis-095° White framework tower Racon
7. **Red and Green Passage Ldg Lts 022°40'**
   49°10'·7N 2°06'·8W
   Front Oc.G.5s10m11M
   Rear 230m from front Oc.R.5s18m12M Synchronised with front. Two thin metal columns, the rear on land and the front on a white painted caisson with a vertical red stripe on the right-hand side of the RoRo berth.
8. **St Helier Harbour Ldg Lts 078°**
   49°10'·7N 2°06'·6W *Front* F.G White column
   Rear 80m from front F.G White column
9. **St Aubin Harbour N Pierhead** 49°11'·2N 2°09'·9W
   Iso.R.4s12m10M Metal column Dir Lt 254°
   DirF.WRG.5m 248°-G-253°-W-255°-R-260° Same structure

Buoys

10. **Desormes Bank** 49°19'·0N 2°17'·9W ✗ card VQ(9)15s
11. **Passage Rock** 49°09'·6N 2°12'·2W ⬆ card VQ
12. **Les Fours** 49°09'·7N 2°10'·1W ⬆ card Q
13. **Ruaudière Rock** 49°09'·8N 2°08'·5W Starboard Fl.G.3s Bell
14. **Diamond Rock** 49°10'·2N 2°08'·54W Port Fl(2)R.6s
15. **East Rock** 49°10'·0N 2°07'·2W Starboard Q.G
16. **Hinguette** 49°09'·4N 2°07'·2W Port Fl(4)R.15s
17. **Small Road** 49°10'·46N 2°07'·13W Port Q.R

Tidal levels referred to chart datum

St Helier 49°11'N 2°07'W
MHWS 11·0 MHWN 8·1 MLWN 4·1 MLWS 1·4
MTL 6·1

Tidal streams

As with all the islands, especially when under sail, the tides are there to be used and from the tidal diagrams (page 134–135) you will see that Jersey, which is roughly rectangular, has a regular pattern of tidal streams. When it is slack east and west, the stream is at maximum on the north and south coast, and roughly vice versa. So, coming from Alderney or Guernsey, should you arrive off the NW corner of Jersey, Grosnez, some 4 hours after HW, 6 hours of fair stream are available to take you up to St Helier ('Town').

Coming from Alderney or Guernsey and bound for Gorey via St Catherine, try to find yourself on the north coast around LW when you will have 4 hours of favourable stream to make port. From St Malo, passing east of the Minquiers, nearly 7 hours of fair stream can be used; depart St Malo an hour before HW so as to arrive near St Helier near LW.

If you study the Admiralty charts you will see that there are many possible approaches to the island but when nearing the island there are nine transits – 7 to St Helier and 2 to Gorey – which are shown on the plans. How much to depart from these transits is easily seen from a quick glance at the Admiralty charts.

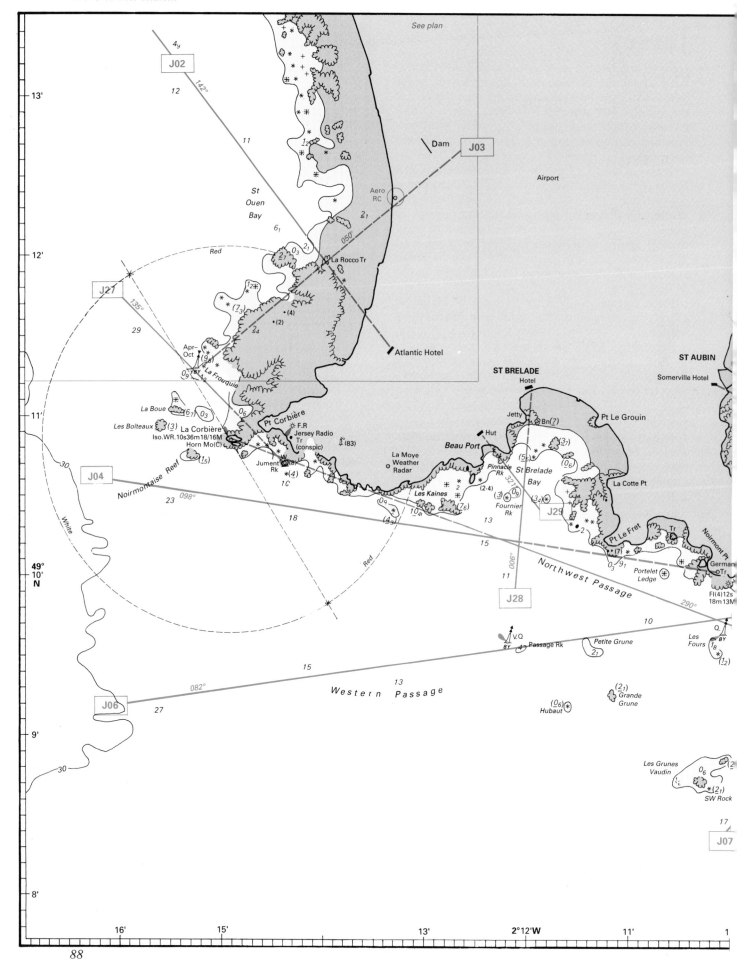

J02

4_y

12

142°

11

*St
Ouen
Bay*

See plan

Dam

J03

Aero
RC

Airport

2_1

6_1

Red

0_3
2_1
2_7

La Rocco Tr

J27

135°

29

1_2

(7_3)

• (4)

• (2)

2_4

Apr-
Oct
(9_4)
BY   *La Frouquie*
0_9

Atlantic Hotel

ST BRELADE

Hotel

ST AUBIN

Somerville Hotel

La Boue
(6_7) 0_3

Les Boîteaux (3)
   La Corbière
Iso.WR.10s36m18/16M
Horn Mo(C)

0_6

Pt Corbière

F.R
Jersey Radio
Tr
(conspic)

(83)

Jetty
1 Bn(7)

(3_1)

Pt Le Grouin

(5_6) *
(0_6)

La Cotte Pt

J04

098°

23

Noirmontaise Reef

(1_5)

Jument
Rk   W
* (4)
$1C$

(8)

*La Moye
Weather
Radar*

Beau Port   Hut

Les Kaines

0_9
*
(4_5)

*Pinnacle
Rk*

2

(2·4)

(7_6)

10_{4I}

*St Brelade
Bay*

(3) 0_9
*Fournier
Rk*

(3_4)*

13

J29

2

Pt Le Fret

(7) *
0_3 9_1

Tr

Noirmont P

German
Tr

White

30

18

Red

321°

15

11

Northwest Passage

290°

Fl(4)12s
18m13M

J28

10

**49°
10'
N**

V.Q
BY 4_7 Passage Rk

Petite Grune
2_1

Les
Fours   Q.
BY
1_8
*

(1_2)

J06

082°

27

15

13

Western   Passage

Hubaut
(0_6)*

(2_1)
*Grande
Grune*

*Les Grunes
Vaudin* 0_6 2

* (2_1)
SW Rock

17

J07

30

13'

12'

11'

9'

8'

16'

15'

13'

2°12'W

11'

1

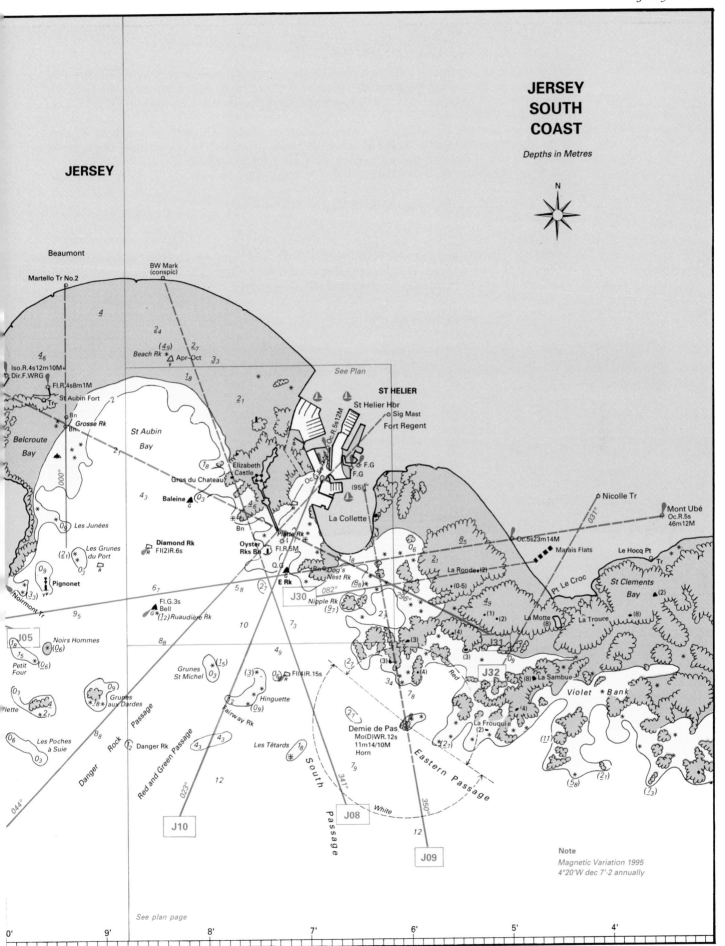

JERSEY
SOUTH
COAST

Depths in Metres

N

Beaumont

BW Mark
(conspic)

Martello Tr No.2

Beach Rk ⚓ Apr-Oct

See Plan

ST HELIER

St Helier Hbr

Iso.R.4s12m10M
Dir.F.WRG
Fl.R.4s8m1M
St Aubin Fort

Oc.R.5s12M

Sig Mast

Fort Regent

Grosse Rk
Bn

St Aubin
Bay

Belcroute
Bay

F.G
F.G

Gros du Chateau

Elizabeth
Castle

Oc.5s

(95)

o Nicolle Tr

Mont Ubé
Oc.R.5s
46m12M

Baleine
G

Les Junées

Oc.5s23m14M

La Collette

Marais Flats

Le Hocq Pt
Tr

Diamond Rk
Fl(2)R.6s

Platte Rk
Fl.R.5M

**Oyster
Rks Bn**

La Ronde

Pt Le Croc

St Clements
Bay

Les Grunes
du Port

Pignonet
YP

Q.G
G
E Rk

Bn Dog's
Nest Rk

082°

La Motte

La Trouce

296°

Noirmont Tr

Fl.G.3s
Bell
Ruaudière Rk

J30

Nipple Rk

La Sambue

J31

La Frouqui

Violet Bank

J05

Noirs Hommes

Petit
Four

Grunes
St Michel

Hinguette

J32

Grunes
aux Dardes

Fl(4)R.15s

Fairway Rk

Red

Demie de Pas
Mo(D)WR.12s
11m14/10M
Horn

Les Poches
à Suie

Danger Rk

Red and Green Passage

Les Tétards

South
Passage

Eastern Passage

J10

023°

341°

White

350°

J08

J09

Danger Rock Passage

Note
Magnetic Variation 1995
4°20'W dec 7'·2 annually

044°

000°

031°

See plan page

St Helier

Platte Rock beacon 49°10'·2N 2°07'·3W

Coming from Alderney or through the Alderney Race, if the conditions are good, steer for Grosnez Point passing between the Desormes Bank buoy and the Pierres de Lecq (or Paternosters Rocks) to enter the Swashway Channel with the stern transit J01 045° (see plan page 95).

From Guernsey or Sark, leave Grosnez Point at least 3M to port to avoid the Rigdon Bank and steer to pass at least 1M to the west of La Corbière LtHo, with the lantern level with the top of the land behind to clear the rocks off La Corbière.

Then either join the NW Passage with Clearing mark J04 099°, or the Western Passage.

1.ST HELIER, NW PASSAGE (8·5m)
(Grade M)

By day

The sea off Grosnez Point is rough with a fresh SW wind against tide and the passage should then be avoided. Otherwise this approach from Guernsey is straightforward and it is only a matter of avoiding the dangers in St Ouen's Bay.

Transit J01 045° – Swashway Channel (or Swatchway) – Great Rock of the Paternosters open of Grosnez Pt on 045° will pass between Rigdon Bank (depth 3·1m over the NE rock) and Moulière Rock (drying 0·6m) leaving it 200m to port.

Clearing mark J02 142°. If you wish to tack into the bay, drying rocks extend a mile off Grand Etaquerel, the conspicuous pyramid of rock 55m high. The clearing mark is: the Atlantic Hotel over La Rocco Tower on 142°. Don't go nearer than ½M from the tower before turning SW.

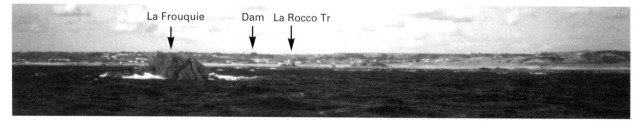

Striking mark J03 050° – La Rocco Tower bearing 050° with the dam open its width to the north

is the striking mark for La Frouquie. To clear this and the other rocks off La Corbière keep a mile off the lighthouse on the NW and W, with the lantern level with the top of the land behind, and run southwards until you can see:

Clearing mark J04 098° – The German tower on Noirmont Point to the right of Le Fret Point.

Then carry on eastwards with the tower well open until well past Les Kaines (drying 8·5m), off the entrance to St Brelade Bay. Then take:

Transit J05 290° – La Corbière LtHo to the right of La Jument white painted rock on 290° as a stern transit.

Just before coming abreast of Noirmont join the Western Passage.

An alternative to clear all dangers west of La Corbière is to put the new La Moye 'Golf Ball' weather radar tower open to the south of La Jument white painted rock on 087°.

By night

Do not pass through the Swashway. The white sector of Grosnez Lt[1] (Fl(2)WR.15s) clears the north end of St Ouen's Bay. Come south, keeping in the white sector of La Corbière Lt[2] (Iso.WR.10s) and leaving the lighthouse at least 1M to port.

When the F.R (on the shore) and La Corbière Lt[2] come in line (079°) identify Noirmont Tower Lt[3] (Fl(4)12s).

Continue south until Noirmont Tower Lt bears 095°, when steer to keep it on this bearing to enter the red sector of La Corbière Lt. As a check, Ruaudière buoy, Fl.G.3s, seen well open of Noirmont Tower light, Fl(4)12s, clears all dangers along the coast.

Identify Passage Rock N card buoy[11] (VQ), Les Fours N card lit buoy[12] (Q) and Ruaudière lit buoy[13] (Fl.G.3s) and, as La Corbière Lt turns from red to white, steer with Ruaudière green light on the port bow and Les Fours white light on the starboard bow to pass midway between Noirmont Pt Lt and Les Fours (leaving Passage Rock buoy ½M to starboard) until the leading lights for the Western Passage[6] (front Oc.5s and rear Oc.R.5s) come in line.

Then follow this transit (082°), leaving Ruaudière green light to starboard, until the Harbour leading lights[7] (front Oc.G.5s, rear Oc.R.5s) are in line (023°) for entry to St Helier.

2. ST HELIER, WESTERN PASSAGE (4m)
(Grade M)

By day

The main transit coming in from the west is:

Transit J06 082° – Grève d'Azette LtHo in line with Dog's Nest Bn. This passes over Passage Rock but if you borrow to the north to leave the Passage Rock buoy to starboard the whole channel then carries 6m.

By night The same transit is used, but since the Dog's Nest Bn is not lit, the mark becomes Mont Ubé Lt[6] (Oc.R.5s46m12M) in line with Grève d'Azette LtHo[6] (Oc.5s23m14M). Mont Ubé's white tower is hard to identify by day.

3. ST HELIER, DANGER ROCK PASSAGE (5·8m) (Grade M)

By day

This passage leaves Danger Rock (1·2m) 400m to starboard and two rocks (depth 0·3m and 0·9m) with Grunes aux Dardes (drying 1·8m) 200m to port so that the line must be held exactly.

Transit J07 044° – Admiralty 1137 has Fort Regent signal mast just open S of breakwater end. The signal mast is hard to identify at a distance but the conspicuous white-painted pierhead control tower makes a good alternative.

By night

The passage is unlit. Use the Red and Green Passage if there is sufficient water over the Fairway Rock (1·2m).

4. ST HELIER, SOUTH PASSAGE (8m) (Grade M)

By day

Once identified with binoculars the marks are conspicuous when a mile from Demie de Pas light tower, in water clear of dangers. With Demie de Pas tower abeam to starboard, Les Tétards rocks (one awash at LW and another depth 1·8m) lie 300m to port.

Transit J08 341°

Transit J08 341° – The black and white vertical stripes on the sea wall between the twin heads of Gros du Château.

By night
Unlit. Use the Eastern Passage.

5. ST HELIER, 'ELECTRIC PASSAGE' (Grade M)

By day
This unofficial passage may be used when approaching from the southeast but must be left, steering 314°, to join the South Passage when 500m from Demie de Pas light tower.

By night
This transit may be used by night if the chimney is floodlit.

Transit J09 350° – Demie de Pas light tower x power station chimney.

6. ST HELIER, EASTERN PASSAGE (7m) (Grade M)

By day
There are no leading marks for this wide passage which joins the Red and Green Passage ½M from Platte Bn.

Keeping in the white sector of Demie de Pas Lt[4] (Mo(D)WR.12s), steer to leave it 300m to starboard and the Hinguette port buoy (Fl(4)R.15s) 400m to port until the marks for the Red and Green Passage appear.

By night
Steer to leave Demie de Pas Lt[4] (Mo(D)WR.12s) 300m to starboard, then steer 314° for the light on St Aubin's pierhead[9] (Iso.R.4s), leaving the Hinguette buoy Lt[16] to port, until the Red and Green Passage lights[7] (front Oc.G and rear Oc.R.5s) are in transit on 023°.

ENTRY TO ST HELIER
Red and Green Passage (Grade M)
(1·2m deep patch at 1M)

Ldg Lts[7] 023° This passage passes over the Fairway Rock (depth 1·2m) between two groups of drying rocks and, near low water, it should only be used for the final entry.

Transit J10 023° – Two thin metal columns, the rear on land and the front on a white painted caisson with a vertical red stripe on the right-hand side of the RoRo berth. Do not confuse the marks with the red painted jibs of a number of cranes inside the harbour.

St Helier Harbour
Photo Patrick Roach

Traffic control

The following signals are displayed from the port control tower:

Signal	Signification
Oc.G or Fl.G	Vessels may enter harbour
Oc.R or Fl.R	Vessels may leave harbour
Oc.G and R or Fl.G and R	No vessel may enter or leave harbour
Q.Y	Vessels under power and under 25m in length may enter or leave, keeping to their starboard side of the pierheads, contrary to the light signal exhibited

Marinas

At the time of writing there were two marinas, La Collette Yacht Basin, on the right before the control tower, with holding berths for visitors, and St Helier Marina in the upper harbour (see plan page 95). Construction of a third marina, west of the Albert Pier, is in progress and may be completed by 1997 (see plan page 95).

La Collette Marina can be entered at most states of tide, but the entrance channel is narrow and has a depth of only 1·8m at MLWS. The port-hand buoys mark the rocky shelf on the east side and can drift at LW in strong winds. Keep close to the west side.

Access to St Helier Marina is possible approximately 3 hours either side of HW. A bottom-hinged gate rises 1·4m above the sill (chart datum +3·6m) to retain depths of 2·3m inside.

When the gate is closed deep-draught yachts should not leave their berths, as depths clear of the pontoons vary and there are shoal areas close to the west, Albert Pier side.

Depth gauges and lights show when entry and exit is possible. The sill gate works automatically and the lights are as on the port control tower, not as road traffic lights:
Green light outside: clear for entry
Red light inside: clear for exit
Red and green together: no entry or exit, or sill gate closed.

When the green light is showing for entry, the red light for exit will also be on, and collision avoidance is the responsibility of those at the helm.

When the marina is closed, yachts should wait in La Collette Yacht Basin or alongside a pontoon on the Albert Pier near the entrance to the marina if there is space.

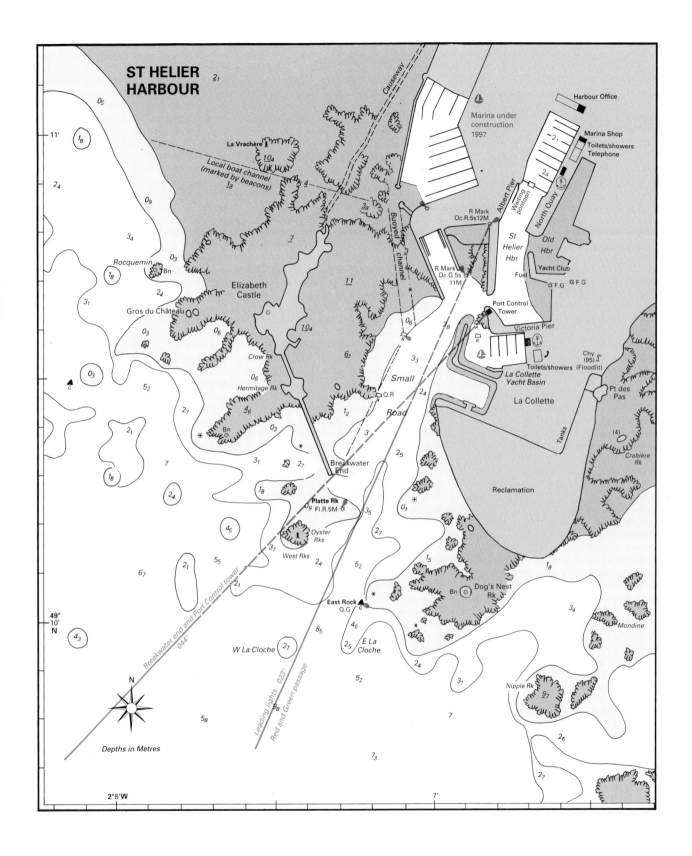

ST HELIER HARBOUR

2₁

Harbour Office

Marina under construction 1997

La Vrachère

Local boat channel (marked by beacons) 1₈

10₄

4

Marina Shop
Toilets/showers
Telephone

2₁

2₄

0₉

2₄

0₉

2₄

3₈

R Mark
Oc.R.5s12M

Albert Pier

Waiting pontoon

North Quay

3₄

7

11

Buoyed channel

St
Helier
Hbr

Old
Hbr

Rocquemin

0₃

Bn

1₈

R Mark
Oc.G.5s
11M

Yacht Club

Fuel

☀ F.G   ☀ F.G

2₄

Elizabeth
Castle

10₄

Port Control
Tower

Gros du Château

0₃

0₆

0₆

R

2₈

Victoria Pier

Chy
(95)

Crow Rk

6₁

3₃

Small

Pt des
Pas

0₃

0₆

La Collette
Yacht Basin

Hermitage Rk

Q.R

2₄

Toilets/showers
(Floodlit)

5₂

4₆

1₂

3

Road

La Collette

(4)

2₇

2₁

Crabière
Rk

7

3₁

2₇

Breakwater
End

2₅

Tanks

Reclamation

1₈

1₈

Platte Rk
Fl.R.5M

3₅

0₉

0₁

2₄

Oyster
Rks

2₄

West Rks

2₇

5₂

1₅

Dog's Nest
Rk

4₆

5₅

6₇

2₁

8₅

East Rock
Q.G

4₆

3₁

Bn

3₄

Mondine

49°
10'
N

4₃

2₁

W La Cloche

9₈

2₇

E La
Cloche

2₅

2₄

Nipple Rk
9₇

2₆

N

5₂

3₁

Leading lights 023°

Red and Green passage

Breakwater end and Port Control tower
044°

Depths in Metres

7₃

7

2₇

2°8'W

7'

St Helier Harbour from the SW prior to construction of the third marina

St Helier Harbour. La Collette Marina in foreground. Ro-Ro
Terminal left

Useful marks around Jersey

Showers and toilets are available at both marinas and there is a food store and laundry close to the St Helier Marina which is open for long hours. The St Helier Yacht Club, on the south pier, welcomes visitors, and chandlers and engineers are close by the club.

Gorey

Starboard buoy 0·74M from breakwater head in approach channel: 49°11'·55N 2°00'·24W. Front leading light[4] on breakwater head: 49°11'·9N 2°01'·3W (Oc.RG.5s8m12M).

Charts

Admiralty *2669, 3655, 1138, 1136.* The old Admiralty *62A* is useful if a photocopy can be obtained from the Hydrographic Office.
Imray *C33A* and *C33B*

Gorey, a large village, with its drying harbour and spectacular Mont Orgueil Castle, is the second port of entry to Jersey and is the nearest to Alderney and France. Consequently, approaches from the north and the southeast will be described, together with the passage from St Helier to Gorey via the Violet Channel.

The difficult passages through the Gutters and over the Violet Bank will be described in a later chapter.

Lights for approaches to Gorey

1. **Grosnez Point** 49°15'·5N 2°14'·7W Fl(2)WR.15s50m19/17M 081°-W-188°-R-241° White hut
2. **Sorel Point** 49°15'·7N 2°09'·4W LFl.WR.7·5s50m15M 095°-W-112°-R-173°-W-230°-R-269°-W-273° Black and white chequered tower
3. **St Catherine breakwater** 49°13'·4N 2°00'·5W Fl.1·5s18m13M White framework tower
4. **Gorey Ldg Lts 298°**49°11'·9N 2°01'·3W
   Front Oc.RG.5s8m12M 304°-R-352°-G-304° White tower on breakwater head.
   Rear 490m from front Oc.R.5s24m8M White square, orange sides, on stone wall

Gorey drying harbour from the SE. *Photo* Patrick Roach

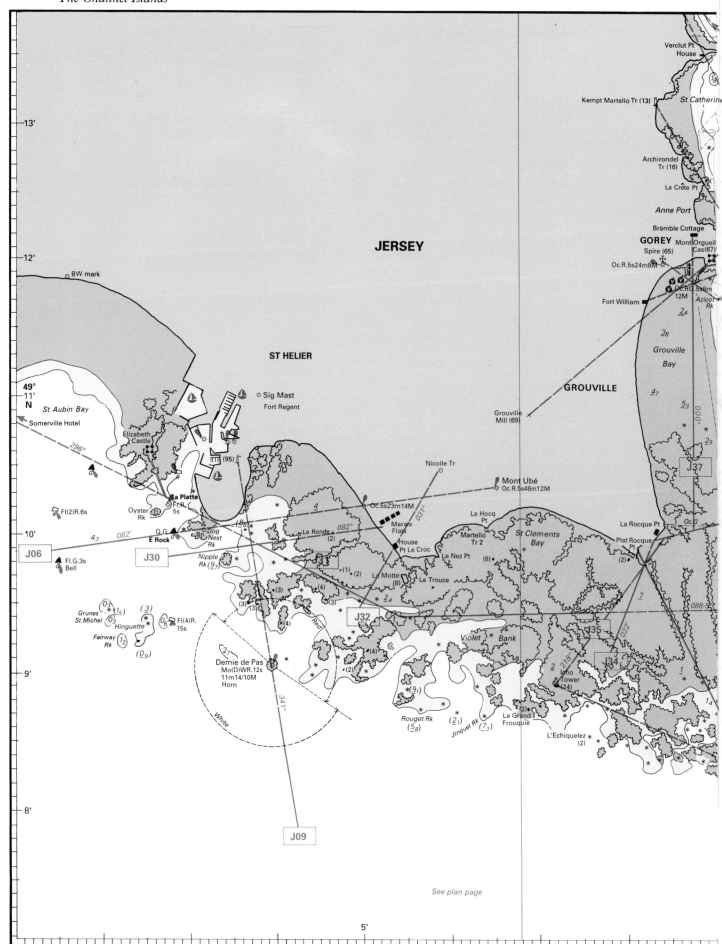

JERSEY

ST HELIER

GROUVILLE

Verclut Pt
House

Kempt Martello Tr (13)

St Catherine

Archirondel
Tr (16)

La Crête Pt

Anne Port

Bramble Cottage

GOREY Mont Orgueil
Spire (65)   Cas (67)
Oc.R.5s24m8M

Fort William   Oc.RG.5s8m
12M   *Azicot*
                 Rk
                 2₄

                 3₈

                 *Grouville
                 Bay*

                 4₇

Grouville   5₃
Mill (69)

                       2₉

                 J37

BW mark

**49°
11'
N**

St Aubin Bay

Somerville Hotel

296°

G

Elizabeth
Castle

(95)

Nicolle Tr

Mont Ubé
Oc.5s46m12M

Le Hocq
Pt

La Rocque Pt
                Oc.G

Martello   *St Clements*
Tr 2   *Bay*

            Plat Rocque
            Pt
            (2)

FI(2)R.6s
R

Oyster
Rk

La Platte
FI.R.
5s

Q.G
E Rock   G

Bn
Dog
Nest
Rk

*Nipple
Rk* (9₇)

La Ronde   *082°*
(2)

Marais
Flats

House
Pt Le Croc

Le Nez Pt   (8)

La Motte
(8)   La Trouce

2₄

7

J06

4₃   *082°*

J30

FI.G.3s
Bell

Grunes
St.Michel 0₃

0₃
1₅

Hinguette

Fairway
Rk   1₂

(3)

0₆ FI(4)R.
15s

(0₉)

(1) (2)

(3)

(3)
(3)

(4)

(4)

(3)

2₄

J32

Violet   *Bank*

2

218°

J35

J34

Icho
Tower
(14)

1

Demie de Pas
Mo(D)WR.12s
11m14/10M
Horn

2₁

341°

White

(4)

(2)

9₁

Rouget Rk
(5₈)

2₁

Jinquet Rk
(7₃)

(2)
La Grand I
Frouquié

L'Echiquelez
(2)

1₄

J09

See plan page

13'

12'

10'

9'

8'

5'

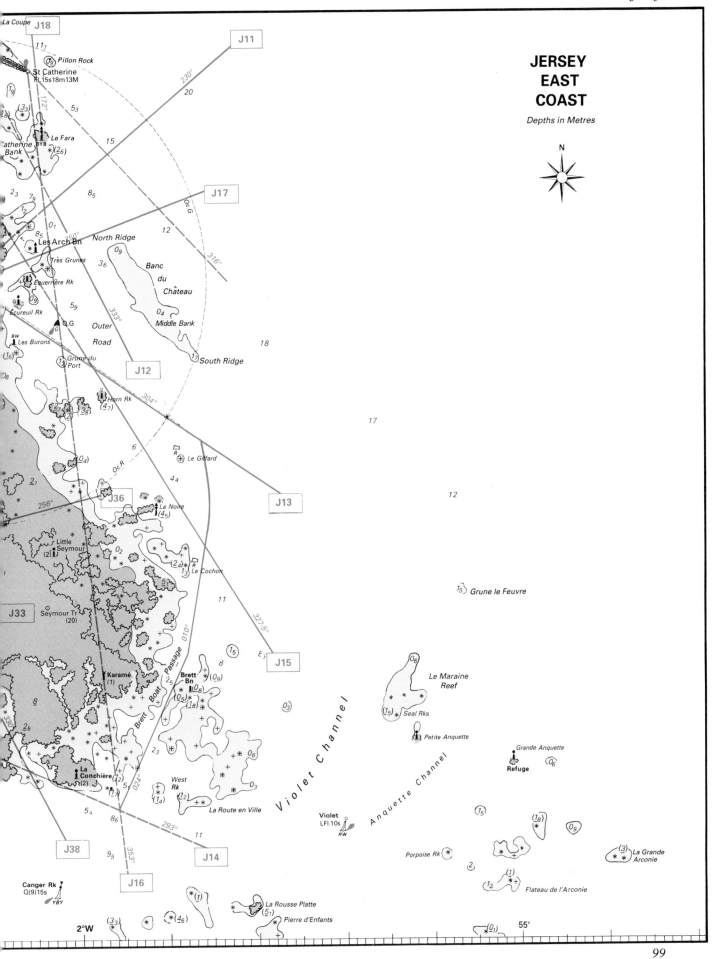

**JERSEY
EAST
COAST**

Depths in Metres

N

La Coupe — **J18**

11₇

(0₉) Pillon Rock

St Catherine
Fl.15s18m13M

(1₉)

(3₃)
*

J11

230°

20

172°

5₃

Le Fara
BYB
(2₆)

Catherine
Bank

15

J17

2₃ 7₉

8₅

12

(1₂)

Oc.G

316°

8₅

0₁

Les Arch Bn

North Ridge

250°

(Très Grunes

0₉)

36

Banc
du
Château

Equerrère Rk

333°

0₄

G(0₉)

Écureuil Rk

5₉

Middle Bank

Outer
Road

18

17₇ South Ridge

BW
Les Burons
(1₆)

Q.G
G

(1₃) Grune du
Port

J12

304°

17

0₈

(2) (3₈)

(4₇) Horn Rk

6

(0₄)

Oc.R

R
Le Giffard

4₄

2₁

J36

La Noire
(4₅)

4₄

J13

256°

Little
Seymour
(2)

0₂

(2₄) R
Le Cochon
1₃

(1₅) Grune le Feuvre

J33

Seymour Tr
(20)

1

5₁

11

327.5°

J15

3₃

1₅

0₆

Le Maraine
Reef

330°

2₆

8

Karamé
(1)

Brett
Bn
(0₉)
(0₈)
(0₅)
(18)

8

010° Brett Boat Passage

1₅ Seal Rks

Petite Anquette

Grande Anquette

0₃

Refuge 0₆

2₃

La Conchière
(1₂)
(1₇)

024°

West
Rk
(1₂)
(1₄)

0₆

0₃

Violet Channel

Anquette Channel

1₅

J38

5₃

86

293°

11

La Route en Ville

Violet
LFl.10s
RW

Porpoise Rk

2

(1₈)

0₉

(3) La Grande
Arconie

J14

9₅

353°

Canger Rk
Q(9)15s
YBY

(1)

La Rousse Platte
(5₁)

Pierre d'Enfants

1₂

(1)

Flateau de l'Arconie

J16

2°W

(3₃)

(4₆)

(0₁)

55'

Buoys
5. **Canger Rock** 49°07'·4N 2°00'·3W ⚑ card Q(9)15s
6. **Frouquier Aubert** 49°06'·2N 1°58'·8W ⚑ card Q(6)+LFl.15s
7. **Violet** 49°07'·9N 1°57'·1W RW Fairway LFl.10s
8. **Gorey Inner Road** 49°11'·5N 2°00'·2W Starboard Q.G

Tidal levels referred to chart datum
St Catherine's Bay 49°13'N 2°01'W MHWS 11·1m
MHWN 8·0m MLWN 4·1m MLWS 1·4m

APPROACH FROM THE NORTH (Grade M)

Depths
The Outer Road, with depths of 6m and more, lies inshore of the Banc du Château with a least depth of 0·4m.

Entry via Transit J13 230° carries 6m.

The Inner Road with Road Rk at depth 3·3m shoals from 8m to 2m south of the starboard beacon on Ecureuil Rk.

Inshore, the channel passes over Azicot Rk drying 2·2m into the harbour which dries from 4m to 6·5m.

Tidal streams
From 5 hours to 2 hours before HW St Helier there will be a fair stream running east along the north coast to La Coupe Pt and then southeast with a maximum of 5 knots springs 3½ hours before HW.

A northerly inshore eddy builds up along the east coast from 3 hours before HW as it does on the west coast and continues until the north-going main stream commences at HW St Helier.

The Channel Pilot Vol II 11th Edition (1952) reports that Le Ruau Channel between Les Dirouilles and the NE coast of Jersey is 2½M wide and clear of dangers but that the confused sea caused by a strong tidal stream setting to windward over the uneven rocky bottom is sometimes so violent as to resemble breakers.

Coming from Alderney or after passing through the Alderney Race, steer for the centre of the north coast of Jersey, passing between the Paternosters (Pierres de Lecq) to the west and Les Dirouilles to the east. The TV mast between Sorel Pt and Bonne Nuit Bay makes a good mark.

Two miles off the coast, with Les Dirouilles abaft the beam to port, steer SE in Le Ruau Channel to leave La Coupe Pt and the end of St Catherine's breakwater 1M to starboard and identify the tower of Grouville Mill as it opens to the south of Mont Orgueil Castle.

Grouville Mill

Transit J11 230° – Grouville Mill open to south of Mont Orgueil Castle. Steer in on this transit with the mill in line with the end of the castle.

At the root of St Catherine's breakwater, above the slipway, is a building with a white end gable and, continuing on the 230° transit the small turret or watch tower on the rounded summit of La Coupe will gradually come into transit over the building.

Transit J12 333° – La Coupe turret over breakwater building. Steer with this as a stern transit to join the Gorey leading marks transit or, if the green buoy in the Inner Road has been positively identified and there is sufficient water to enter the harbour, steer to round the buoy, leaving it to starboard.

The harbour dries 6·5m. The leading lines for entry pass directly over Azicot Rock (drying 2·2m) but this should present no hazard if there is sufficient water to enter the harbour.

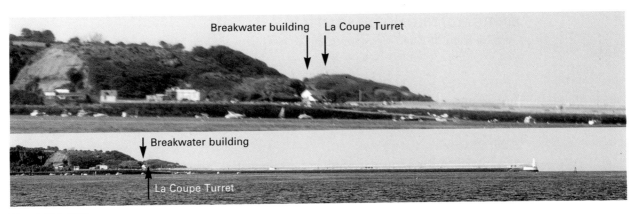

Transit J12 333°

The leading marks for entry by day are:

Transit J13 304° – Gouray church spire (Gouray church not Gorey) over the white patch on the end of the pier on 304°.

For night entry on 298°, the front light4 (Oc.RG.5s) is situated on a white framework tower on the end of the pier above the white patch, while the rear light (Oc.R.5s) is over a white stone wall with vertical dayglow orange borders.

Note that the dividing line between the northern red and the southern green sector of the front leading light lies along the daylight transit of 304°, and if approaching at night it is preferred to have the rear light open to the left, but not so far that the front light turns green.

APPROACH FROM THE SOUTHEAST (Grade M)

Tidal streams east of Jersey and Iles Chausey

The streams rotate anticlockwise. In general, the northerly stream to the east and northeasterly stream to the southeast of Jersey commences 1 hour before HW St Helier. Off Granville the northerly set commences 2½ hours before HW.

The stream increases to a maximum of 3 knots at springs, 2–4M east of Jersey and 2 knots or less to the south. The stream then swings to the west, with a southrunning eddy close inshore to the east coast of Jersey at HW+4.

By HW+5 it is running SW at 1–2 knots at springs, swinging SE and increasing up to 3·4 knots at springs north of the Minquiers and Chausey. At HW−2½ it is running ESE, with a north-running eddy close inshore to the east coast of Jersey, and by HW−1½ the stream turns NE and slackens.

Departure over the sill at Granville is possible 3 hours either side of HW St Helier.

Coming from Granville, navigate to pass east or west of Iles Chausey and either, steer for the Bas Jourdan E card buoy Q(3)10s Whis (49°06'·9N 1°44'·1W), via the Entrée de la Déroute, or for the Canger Rk W card buoy Q(9)15s (49°07'·4N 2°00'·3W) to enter the Violet Channel. (See Admiralty chart 2669).

From the Bas Jourdan buoy, leaving it to port, steer 295° until Mont Orgueil Castle can be identified, then hold it on 295° and identify the harbour leading marks (see J13 above).

Come onto the leading line 304° to enter the harbour if there is sufficient depth, or to anchor in the Inner Road.

For depths see northern approach.

APPROACH FROM THE SOUTH

Coming from St Malo it is convenient to pass between the Minquiers and Iles Chausey to take the Violet Channel (see below).

APPROACH FROM THE WEST

Approach via the Violet Channel (Grade M), the Anquette Channel (Grade M) or the Brett Boat Passage (Grade EC).

Tidal streams

An E to SE stream along the south coast commences 5 hours before HW St Helier, while the stream is running SE at 3 knots springs off Gorey. At HW−3½ the south coast stream may be running at 3 knots with 3 knots or more off Gorey.

At HW−2½ the south coast stream is slackening and a north-going eddy is building up inshore along the east coast of Jersey. This would be a good time to take the Violet Passage and approach Gorey on a rising tide.

Leave St Helier by the South Passage and, when the Demie de Pas light tower is abeam to port, steer 105°, leaving Icho Tower 1M to port, to identify Canger Rk W card buoy Q(9)15s and La Conchière beacon with its topmark deliberately bent towards the north (see photo below).

Steer to pass midway between La Conchière Bn and Canger Rk buoy. Then keeping:

Transit J14 293° – Icho Tower open to the left of La Conchière, to clear West Rock and La Route en Ville.

Identify the Violet Channel RW safe-water buoy (LFl.10s) and steer to pass it on either side and endeavour to identify the next marks.

These are: The small turret/watch tower on La Coupe Pt, nearly 7M distant, open east of Verclut Pt on 332°.

Refer to Transit J12 page 100 which is virtually the same, as Verclut Pt runs down behind the breakwater house.

Hold this transit to enter Gorey Outer Road.

In poor visibility, from a point 600m NE of Violet buoy steer 332°, leaving Petite Anquette faded orange beacon with 'PA' topmark and Seal Rks (drying 1·5m) 800m to starboard.

Proceeding on this course, Le Cochon red can buoy and La Noire E card Bn will be left to port, and, on approaching the leading line for entry to Gorey, Le Giffard red can buoy should be left close to port.

Do not attempt this approach by night.

An alternative transit which leaves Le Cochon buoy, La Noire Bn and Horn Rk Bn to port and Le Giffard red can buoy to starboard is with:

Transit J15

Transit J15 327·5° – Archirondel RW Martello tower x *Kempt Tower behind it or open to the left.*

The towers may not at first be conspicuous but it is sufficient to leave Le Cochon buoy, La Noire Bn and Horn Rk Bn 400m to port and Le Giffard buoy 400m to starboard.

ANQUETTE CHANNEL

Northeast of the Violet buoy is a clean channel ¾M wide between the Grande Anquette and Petite Anquette beacons. The Grande Anquette Bn is conical with a black base, at LW, a faded yellow (1994) top and a white staff with a black sphere as topmark, while the Petite Anquette Bn is a narrow column, faded orange with a black conical base and a staff with 'PA' topmark.

This channel may be taken as an alternative to the Violet Channel by steering 055° from the Violet buoy. Midway between Petite and Grande Anquette steer 020° with due regard for the tidal stream until Gorey bears 298°, then steer for the harbour.

BRETT BOAT PASSAGE

With sufficient water and good visibility the Brett Passage, with rocks drying 2m or more on either side, may be used as an alternative to the Violet Channel. It should be noted that the Brett beacon can be submerged and so present a hazard on a high spring tide.

With Canger Rk buoy abeam to starboard steer for the position where:

Transit J14 293° – Icho Tower is open south of La Conchière Bn, and:

Transit J16 353° – Karamé Bn is just on the end of St Catherine's breakwater. (In the photo Karamé Bn is shown to the left of the breakwater head.)

From this point steer 024° to leave Brett Bn, a metal framework with 'B' topmark, 300m to starboard. Then, a course of 010° should leave Le Cochon red can buoy close to port and, locating Le Giffard red can buoy and leaving it 300m to port, identify the leading marks for entry to Gorey.

Facilities

Fuel, water, engineers, chandlers, showers and toilets, banks, post office, hotels, pubs, shops, bus to Town, car hire and taxis.

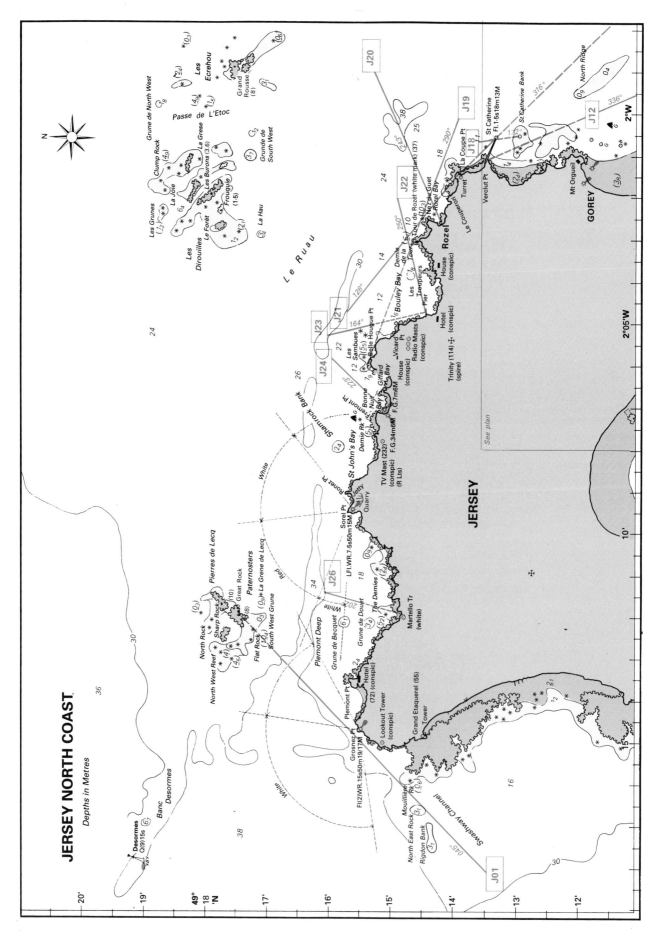

JERSEY NORTH COAST

Depths in Metres

Gorey to St Helier northabout
(Generally Grade M)

In fine weather, with the absence of fresh winds from the northern sector a visit to the north coast of Jersey is worthwhile, revealing an interesting coastline with four small harbours and no dangers more than ½M offshore.

Charts

Admiralty *3655, 1138, 1136, 1137*
Imray *C33A*

Lights

It is not assumed that this passage will be taken at night but, working from east to west, the following lights are available:
1. **St Catherine breakwater** 49°13'·4N 2°00'·5W Fl.1·5s18m13M White framework tower
2. **Rozel Dir Lt 245°** 49°14'·3N 2°02'·7W DirF.WRG.11m5M 240°-G-244°-W-246°-R-250°
3. **Bonne Nuit Bay Ldg Lts 223°** 49°15'·1N 2°07'·0W
   Front F.G.7m6M Pole over white patch on end of jetty
   Rear 170m from front F.G.34m6M Dayglow orange and white pole
4. **Sorel Point** 49°15'·7N 2°09'·4W LFl.WR.7·5s50m 15M 095°-W-112°-R-173°-W-230°-R-269°-W-273° Black and white chequered round concrete tower
5. **Grosnez Point** 49°15'·5N 2°14'·7W Fl(2)WR.15s50m 19/17M 081°-W-188°-R-241° White hut

Tidal levels referred to chart datum

Rozel 49°14'N 2°02'W MHWS 10·7m MHWN 8·2m
MLWN 3·9m MLWS 1·6m

Tidal streams

For a general picture refer to the tidal diagrams on page 134.

At HW−1 St Helier the offshore stream is easterly but a weak inshore eddy occurs running NW off St Catherine's breakwater and west as far as Bonne Nuit Bay. The easterly stream continues along the western half of the north coast until HW+2 by which time the offshore stream will be running WNW at up to 3½ knots at springs.

From HW+3 to HW+6 the north coast inshore stream runs west, at not more than 2 knots, after which a weak easterly eddy commences along the western half of the north coast. By HW−5 the stream will be easterly along the north coast.

For the streams from Grosnez Pt to St Helier see page 87.

From the above it is seen that the best time to leave Gorey is at HW St Helier. There will then be enough water to leave between Les Arch BW Bn with A topmark to the north and Equerrière Rk Bn with its 'fish tail' topmark to the south.

Rounding the pierhead, identify the red-roofed house built on the remains of Fort William and, keeping 400m off the breakwater, come round to the NE until:

Transit J17 250° – Fort William house is just open to the south of the end of the pier.

Steer with this as a stern transit until St Catherine's breakwater head is in transit with La Coupe turret on 316°.

Course may then be altered to leave the breakwater head 100m to port or, if desired, to enter the northern half of St Catherine's Bay.

St Catherine's breakwater

Breakwater head 49°13'·4N 2°00'·58W

Built in the mid-19th century it was, as with the breakwater at Braye on Alderney, intended to shelter the entire British fleet. Work proceeded without a thorough survey and, after completion, the bay was found to be silting, too shallow and encumbered with rocks to accommodate a number of large warships.

Do not secure to the breakwater which is foul throughout its length. Anchor clear south of the breakwater and any moorings, in 3m or more. There is a landing slip at the root with small-craft moorings and a sailing club, a café and a bus service to town.

The slip and boathouse for the St Catherine's *Atlantic 21* inshore lifeboat is just south of the landing slip (drying 4·7m) by the Martello tower midway between the northern breakwater and Archirondel RW Martello tower by the unfinished southern breakwater. NE of Archirondel Tower is a newly established fish farm marked out by buoys.

Anchoring in 4m 200m NE of the above-water rock (7m) off La Crête Pt, investigate by dinghy the drying coves either side of the point. The southern cove, Anne Port, has a landing slip.

Continuing north
(Grade EC)

Chart

Admiralty *1136* is preferable but *3665* could be used with care for a thorough exploration.

Continuing north, leave St Catherine's breakwater head close to port, passing inside Pillon Rk (depth 0·9m) and steer with:

Transit J18 172° – Le Fara E card framework Bn open of the end of the breakwater to clear Coupe Rk (2·7m) and Brayes Rks (drying 1·8m) off La Coupe Pt.

La Fara

Photo J18

Rozel   Tour de Rozel

Transit J19 290° – When Belle Hougue Pt is open of the conspicuous Tour de Rozel on 290° course may be altered to follow this transit to approach the drying harbour of Rozel.

ROZEL 49°14'·3N 2°02'·57W

This delightful fishing harbour, sheltered from all except a NE blow, is full of small craft on drying moorings behind the pier. It is possible to anchor outside and then perhaps, with local agreement, enter and dry out inside.

The entrance is narrow between the pierhead and a W card beacon marking the end of a rocky plateau stretching to the east of the harbour. Small red and green buoys mark the approach channel. Entry at half tide is possible and the pier dries about 1·5m.

5-window gable

Transit J20 243° – Enter with the conspicuous white end-gable with a circle of five windows open to the left of the white patch on the end of the pier.

Entry by night is possible, but not advised, using the narrow white sector of the Dir.F.GWR light on 245°.

Facilities

Rozel is a small fishing village with a gift shop, a pub, restaurants, an hotel and an hourly bus to town (30 minutes).

The photo shows the harbour and slip with the rear leading mark, the end-gable with five windows.

Continuing west

Continuing west, leave Rozel on the 243° transit and when the Tour de Rozel bears west, steer 290° to leave Demie de la Tour, a rock drying 6·1m off the Tour de Rozel, 500m to port.

If a visit to Bouley Bay is not intended, northeast of Belle Hougue Pt lie Les Sambues, drying 3·4m and 5·5m, which are considered to be a major hazard on the north coast.

On Admiralty *1136* the clearing marks are the Turret on La Coupe on the north end of Tour de Rozel on 124°.

When the area was visited in 1994 this transit, although looking safe on Admiralty *1136*, appeared to pass too close to Les Sambues and the transit shown in J21 was preferred.

Stern transit J21 128° – La Coupe turret over a rock drying 10·3m north of Nez du Guet (shown on the old Admiralty *62B* but not shown on Admiralty *1136*).

This rock may cover at HWS but at this state of tide there should be adequate water over Les Sambues, and a transit with the turret open of the north of the Tour de Rozel will be safe.

Clearing marks for Les Sambues are: either Bouley Bay pier or Bonne Nuit Bay pier open of the land.

BOULEY BAY (Pierhead 49°14'·5N 2°04'·7W) is the anchorage before Belle Hougue Pt, with a fishing pier and small-craft moorings somewhat exposed to winds from the NE quadrant.

Transit J22 250° – Steer in between the Tour de Rozel and Les Troupeurs (rocks with 1·8m over them) with the right side of Fort Lester over the white patch on the pier end.

Anchorage

Anchor on sand in 2·5m clear of the moorings, 200m SE of the pierhead. The harbour dries 1·6m.

Facilities

The harbour offers a pub, hotel and buses to Town (30 minutes).

Continuing west

Leaving Bouley Bay to continue westwards, Les Sambues drying 3·4m and 5·5m present a hazard to be avoided.

The clearing marks, with due consideration to tidal stream, are:

Transit J23 164° – The root of Bouley pier in line with Vicard Point on 164°.

When clear to the north of Les Sambues steer west, with the option of a visit to Bonne Nuit Bay.

BONNE NUIT HARBOUR
49°16'·5N 2°07'W

This drying harbour is similar in design to Rozel but the shelter from NW winds provided by Fremont Point is not as great as that given to Rozel by the Tour de Rozel and Nez du Guet.

Cheval Rk (Chevel Rk on Admiralty *1136*), an above-water rock 400m ENE of the pierhead and marked by a radar reflector on a pole, has a spur extending 200m to the north which is left to port on entry with:

Transit J24 223° – The leading marks in transit and the white house on the ridge open to the right of the white patch on the pierhead. Note the bus passing in front of the rear mark and the TV mast far right.

A night approach is possible with both the leading marks lit, F.G.6M.

Anchorage

Behind the pier the harbour is full of chain mooring trots on sand for small craft and there is no room for visitors. The foreshore of the bay is rocky and visiting yachts should not attempt to take the ground.

Anchor clear of any fishermen's buoys in 2m midway between the pierhead and Cheval Rk (see photo below).

Bonne Nuit
anchorage

Facilities

Hotel, kiosk, pub and a bus service to town (30 minutes).

Leaving

Leaving Bonne Nuit anchorage, steer north and identify the starboard buoy guarding Demie Rk, drying 5·2m, 600m north of Fremont Pt. Proceeding west this buoy should be left to port, steering to pass between the buoy and Shamrock Bank should there be any disturbance over the 2·4m rock on the south side of the bank.

Leave Ronez Pt with its jetty and conspicuous quarry ½M to port and, if a brief visit is intended, steer to pick up the leading marks for:

GREVE DE LECQ 49°15'N 2°12'W

Grève de Lecq has a popular bathing beach but the stone pier is destroyed and there is no fishing activity.

The Demies (drying 5·2m) lie 600m north of the eastern arm of the bay. There is only ½m at LWS between the Demies and the beach to the south but from 2m to 4m may be found between them and the ruined pier.

Approach from the northeast

Clearing marks J25 235° (not shown on plan) – The left gable of the lower house under the right gable of the left-hand higher house clears the rocks off the point and:

Clearing marks J25

Martello Tr   Hotel des Pierres

Clearing marks J26 202° – The white Martello tower x *the Hotel des Pierres* will leave the Demies to starboard. The picture shows the hotel well open to the right of the tower to the left of the picture, with the houses for J25 in the centre and the Demies exposed right centre.

Anchorage

Admiralty *1136* shows a cable running out from the slipway. An anchorage should be found 200m NE of the ruined pier which, if continuing westward, can be left by steering out with the Martello tower on a stern bearing of 165°.

Facilities

Not much; a beach café, a couple of pubs, and a bus to Town.

Grève de Lecq is the last anchorage to be visited on the north coast after which, steering out to leave Plemont Pt 800m to port and, if the water inshore is not disturbed, Grosnez Pt 200m to port, the Swashway Channel may be taken to return to St Helier (see page 90).

La Corbière Boat Passage, St Brelade Bay and St Aubin

Charts

Admiralty *3655* and *1137*. The old Admiralty *810* (corrected to 1974) is useful if a photocopy can be obtained from the Hydrographic Office.

La Corbière lighthouse 49°10'·85N 2°14'·95W (Grade EC)

The Boat Passage between La Corbière Rock and the Noirmontaise Reef can be taken with caution and only in calm weather but is not recommended during a first visit. In April 1995 one of the French ferries, which used the passage frequently, struck La Frouquie and the harbour office do not recommend it.

Lights

No lights are given as this passage should only be attempted by day.

Tidal streams

Between LW St Helier and HW−2½ the tidal stream is favourable, running south to La Corbière and then eastwards along the coast to St Helier.

Coming from the north, the main danger is La Frouquie (drying 9·8m) which should be left 200m to port. As a result of the accident with the ferry this rock is now guarded during the summer months by a W card buoy. In avoiding La Frouquie one is liable to pass over rocks awash at chart datum.

Photo J03 page 90 shows the striking marks for La Frouquie, which dries 9·8m, and is therefore exposed at most states of the tide.

Approach

Steer for La Corbière lighthouse on 148°, keeping an eye on La Rocco Tower and the dam (J03) and identify the conspicuous white patch on Jument Rk (8m) seen between the lighthouse and Pt Corbière.

On reaching:

Transit J27 135° – White patch on Jument Rk between the two heads of Les Jumelles (drying about 9m and 8m), steer on this transit, with due attention to the tidal stream. Near LWS steer with the white patch to the left of centre between Les Jumelles, as in the photo, to avoid the two rocks almost awash.

Once 200m south of La Frouquie, steer just to the east (left) of the lighthouse and when 400m off the Corbière Rock, which is steep-to, alter to starboard and steer round it at a distance of 200m. When the lighthouse bears 045°, steer out on 130° until:

Clearing mark J04 098° (page 91) – The German tower on Noirmont Point well to the right of Le Fret Point. Then carry on with the Noirmont Pt light tower bearing 100° until, after leaving Les Kaines (drying 8·5m) to port, looking astern:

Transit J05 290° (page 91) – La Corbière LtHo to the right of La Jument white painted rock on 290° as a stern transit.

At this point it would be convenient to enter St Brelade Bay.

If entry is not intended, continue on to join the Western Passage for St Helier (see page 92).

ST BRELADE BAY
Rocquet Bn 49°10'·97N 2°11'·9W

This is an attractive bay with a popular bathing beach. There are a number of rocks in its centre and mouth and, because the number of new houses built behind the black and white chequered Martello tower confuses the transit for entry on the east side, entry should be into the western half of the bay.

Coming from La Corbière, Les Kaines group of rocks drying 10·4m, 8·5m and 7·6m to the west of the bay will be conspicuous except at HW but Fournier Rk (drying 0·9m), further into the bay and situated one third of the way across the mouth (see plan) may be a danger near LW. An uncorrected Admiralty *1137* will show the rock as drying 3m as the chart was published before the height of the rock was reduced to drying 0·9m by blasting.

500m to the east of Fournier Rk lies Fourche Rk (drying 3·4m) and the transit passes between the two rocks.

Transit J28 006° – The right side of the hotel x the white patch on the end of the jetty.

Some Jerseymen use the conspicuous pink house on the skyline x the white patch, a good mark as long as the house has not been repainted. This transit passes closer to Fournier Rk.

Hold Transit J28 until 400m from the jetty, leaving Fournier du Havre (drying 5·5m) and a further group of lesser rocks to starboard and, when 300m off the jetty, alter to starboard and come to anchor, on soundings, south of Rocquet Bn.

At LWS it may be necessary to anchor on Transit J28 when Fournier du Havre is abeam.

The conspicuous pinnacle rock in Beau Port, a tiny sandy cove on the west side of St Brelade Bay, which itself deserves a visit, makes a useful mark when entering from the east.

Transit J29 321° – Pinnacle Rock x hut on skyline.

Come in on this transit and, unless intending to visit Beau Port, turn onto Transit J28 006° when the marks are in line.

ST AUBIN BAY

This shallow bay, bounded by Noirmont Pt on the west and Elizabeth Castle 1½M to the east, has been used as an anchorage for many years and is still used by yachts when St Helier is full. However, while appearing to afford shelter from the west, the anchorage can become uncomfortable in bad weather.

The Martello tower at Beaumont (see Admiralty *3655* and *1137*) is no longer painted white and the Sillette Passage is not now used as an approach to St Helier. It can however be used, after passing Noirmont Tower in the Western Passage if the tower and Grosse Rk white beacon can be identified.

Leaving Pignonet S card Bn to port, steer in on 000° with Grosse Rk Bn x Martello Tr No. 2.

This transit leaves Les Grunes du Port (drying 2·1m) 200m to starboard and passes over Les Junées a 0·9m patch. If tide permits, St Aubin Harbour may be entered by holding the transit, leaving three rocks to starboard, turning to starboard when 200m from Grosse Rk white Bn and rounding the north head of St Aubin Fort pier, keeping 400m clear of the eastern end of the fort.

For a less troublesome entry to the bay from the west:

On the Western Passage Transit, (J06 082° page 92), when Pignonet S card Bn is abeam to port steer 065°, leaving Les Grunes du Port (red can buoy) to port and round Diamond Rk (red can lit buoy), leaving it to port to enter the bay.

THE GUTTERS
(Grade H)

The passage from St Helier over the Violet Bank to La Rocque Harbour and on to Gorey is included for interest. It should on no account be attempted by visitors unless accompanied by an experienced local who is prepared to accept full responsibility. I am most grateful to two of them who took me through in their own boats.

Admiralty *1137* (1979) and *1138* (1984) disagree on some features in the area and locals still use Admiralty *62A* and *62B*.

One traditional entrance to the Gutters from St Helier has been blocked by reclamation south of La Collette and a leading mark obscured.

A tidal level of more than 8m is necessary for the passage of vessels with a draught of up to 1·5m.

Departing from St Helier and leaving East Rock starboard buoy (E La Cloche on Admiralty *1137*) to port, steer towards Demie de Pas light tower.

Identify La Ronde (2m) rock and the four conspicuous Le Marais Flats tower blocks.

Steer in on:

Transit J30 082° – La Ronde x right-hand side of right-hand tower block.

When the Somerville Hotel in St Aubin comes over the black and white stripes on the Elizabeth Castle breakwater end, alter onto this:

La Ronde

Transit J30
Photo AGW Clarke

Somerville Hotel

Somerville Hotel

Stern transit J31 296° – Somerville Hotel ✕ Elizabeth Castle breakwater end.

Hold this transit and, as Le Marais Flats come abeam, look for the white Nicolle Tower on the skyline and a house with a grey tiled roof between the white gable ends of two other houses, on the shore.

Nicole Tr

Breast mark J32 031° – Nicolle Tower ✕ grey tiled roof.

The next marks are: Seymour Tower (49°09'·50N 2°00'·37W), a stone tower 20m high and La Conière (3m on *1137* and 1·5m on *1138*), a white painted rock with a 'C' topmark on a short iron pole.

Transit J33 088·5° – Seymour Tower open to the south of La Conière.

According to chart Admiralty *1137* and the old *62B*, the stern transit J31 should be held past the breast mark J32 until J33 is on. This will just clear a rock drying 8·8m northeast of La Sambue (height 8m).

Once J33 is on, follow the transit to approach La Conière until Icho Tower bears 180°. Then change course to leave La Conière 100m to starboard, slowly bringing Seymour Tower in line and then open to the north of La Conière.

Approaching La Conière, La Rocque Point will open from behind the breakwater.

Identify the building with the tallest roof in the group of houses on the point and turn towards the breakwater on:

Transit J34 022° – Tall roof ✗ *white patch on end of breakwater.*

Steer on this transit and, 100m from the breakwater head, turn out to leave it 20m to port.

If intending to carry on to Gorey, do not turn into the harbour but cross it with the stern transit:

Transit J35 218° – Icho Tower just open of the breakwater head.

The rock shown as above water (1m) on Admiralty *1137* is shown as drying 8m on *1138* and drying 38ft (11·58m) on *62A*. Proceed across the harbour with caution and search for the next, somewhat unusual marks.

At the top of a slip at the north end of the harbour is a red lifebelt and above it an orange daymark. The stern transit, which must be held accurately is:

Transit J36 256° – Orange daymark (close by a public call box), over the end of the sea wall, with half the lifebelt concealed behind the wall. The photo was taken slightly south of the transit and the whole lifebelt is exposed.

This transit, if held for 1½M, leads clear out to seaward.

Alternatively, to steer up to Gorey, leave J36 when:

Transit J37 000° – Bramble Cottage ✗ *Gorey pierhead light.*

With an 8m tide, Admiralty *62A* indicates that there is more water than does Admiralty *1138* and this is an accepted route to arrive on when there is sufficient water to enter Gorey Harbour.

DEMIE DE PAS ENTRY AND LA MOTTE OR GREEN ISLAND DRYING ANCHORAGE

While there is no transit for this channel, it is sufficiently wide to permit entry on a single bearing.

From a position 400m northwest of Demie de Pas light tower, steer for the centre of Green Island (La Motte on Admiralty *1137*) on 065°. This course will leave Bailhache

Transit J37

(height 4m) 200m to port, Round Rouget (just exposed at HW) 200m to starboard and leads to the position where the Breast mark J32 (page 113) crosses the Transit J31 (page 113).

From this point the passage in the Gutters to La Rocque may be followed, or a turn to starboard onto 085° leads to a drying anchorage on sand 200m SW of Green Island.

LA ROCQUE HARBOUR

This interesting, drying harbour contains a number of small fishing boats which, when afloat, use a channel with a single transit giving an exit clear out to sea.

Stern Transit J38 330° – Southwestern slip just open of the breakwater head.

Photo J38A shows the channel as seen from the slipway.

Photo J38A

Les Ecrehou

Before 1607 the spelling was L'Escrehou which accounts for the absence of an 's' at the end of the name!

In 1203 these rocks were a gift to a Norman monastery on condition that a light be built for ships and a chapel for souls. 106 years later the Abbot of Valrichier, to avoid paying *droit de moulinage*, proved that the priory of the Ecrehou was maintained by revenue from a mill near Rozel. The money, he said, was essential to pay for a daily mass for the king and, of course, to maintain the lighthouse. The seigneur of the manor of Rozel must have relented and let him off paying. The priory ruins still exist on Maître Ile.

Over 100 years ago, when returning to Jersey from France in windless weather, a sailing ship was holed on the reef at low water. The thirty passengers, all women, just managed to crowd on a small rock while the crew swam to safety on Marmotière. Night fell, the tide rose and when morning came the rock was bare. Carried on a sullen winters gale the screams can still be heard when the spring tides wash over a rock called Prières des Femmes.

And there is still no light on Ecrehou.

From Rozel to Ecrehou is only 5M and it is not surprising that, though smaller than the Minquiers, the island is visited more often. The houses, about a dozen, are well kept and their States leases are much prized by Jersey yachtsmen.

The area is very rough at springs with a SE wind, and a first visit should be made at neap tides, in calm weather, in good visibility and with no risk of fog.

For a first visit, a good time to arrive is about HW−2, when the stream is fairly slack and the tide is still rising. Owners of huts on Marmotière aim to arrive at half tide down, when the shingle ridge joining the two islands is uncovered. It is easier then to row ashore and, if intending to stay, the channels to the pool may be inspected at low water.

Charts

Admiralty *3655* has the largest scale recently available. The old *62a* (to 1974) is out of print, but a photocopy might be obtainable from the Hydrographic Office.

Lights

There are no lights and entry should only be attempted by day in good visibility.

Tidal levels referred to chart datum

49°17'N 1°56'W MHWS 10·9m MHWN 8·4m
MLWN 3·8m MLWS 1·3m MTL 6·1m

Tidal streams

In the channel running NNW to Marmotière and round the eastern side. Reference St Helier:

HW−1 the stream is slack

HW NNW 1·0–2·0 increasing to 2·5–5·0 or more then decreasing to:

HW+4 NNW 1·0–2·0

HW+5 NNW 0·5–1·0

HW+6 SSE 1·0–2·0 increasing to 2·0–5·0 and even 6·0 E of Marmotière, then decreasing.

See plan for detail.

Depths

The anchorage and moorings SE of Marmotière can be approached at all states of tide with a least depth at the moorings of 1·5m LWS. The pool has recently been silting, the sand is ridged, and deep-draught vessels who cannot take the ground should enter with caution, if at all. One metre may be found in places to the west at LWS but there is more water at neaps. A reef of *sargassum muticum* (Japanese seaweed) was reported in the pool in 1995.

E03. Looking NW over Marmotière near low water

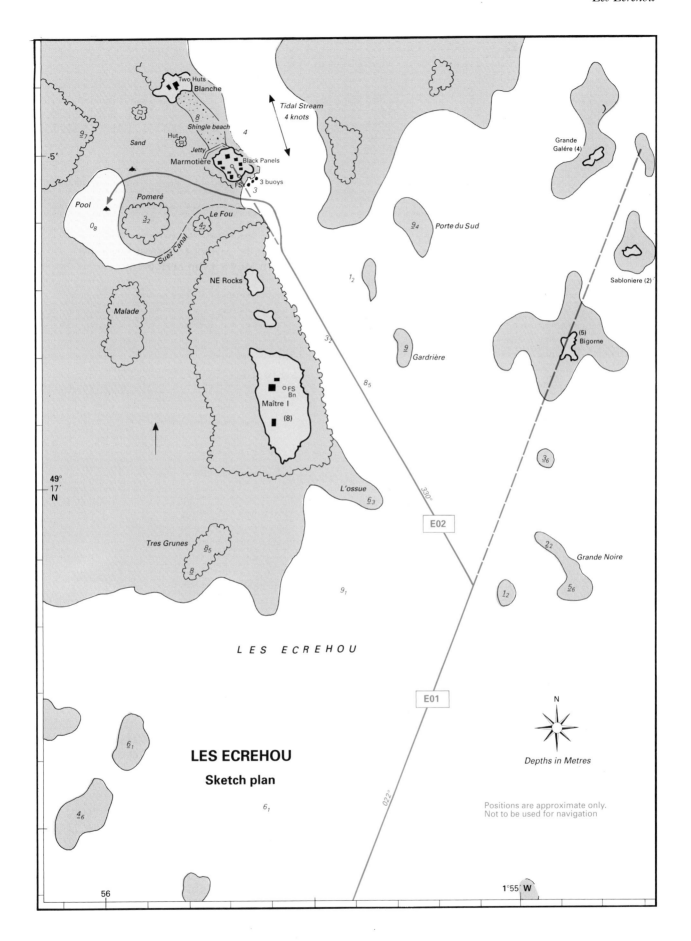

Two Huts
Blanche

Shingle beach
4

Sand
Hut
Jetty
Marmotière
Black Panels
FS
3 buoys
3

Tidal Stream
4 knots

Grande
Galére (4)

9_7

·5'

Pool
0_8

Pomeré
3_2

Le Fou
4_2

Suez Canal

NE Rocks

9_4 Porte du Sud

Sabloniere (2)

1_2

Malade

9 Gardrière

(5)
Bigorne

FS
Bn
Maître I
(8)

8_5

3_2

3_6

49°
17'
N

L'ossue
6_3

330°

E02

2_2
Grande Noire

5_6

Tres Grunes
8_5

8

9_1

1_2

L E S   E C R E H O U

E01

N

6_1

LES ECREHOU

Sketch plan

6_1

Depths in Metres

Positions are approximate only.
Not to be used for navigation

022°

4_6

56

1°55' **W**

Approach (Grade M)

Coming from Rozel, Gorey or the Violet Channel, make a position 49°15'·3N 1°56'W where the mast beacon on Maître Ile will bear 010°.

High Water

Gde Galère   Bigorne   Sablonière

Low Water

Transit E01 022° – Bigorne pinnacle rock between Grande Galère and Sablonière.

Follow this course, leaving La Ronde Selhère (drying 2·7m) 200m to starboard and La Vraic (drying 1·8m) 400m to port.

When Marmotière is open of Maître Ile alter to port to come onto:

Transit E02 330° – Two black panels on with the Marmotière flagstaff with a white painted rock below.

This course leads to the anchorage off Marmotière where there are some moorings.

At LWS the pinnacle of Bigorne is still conspicuous although many other rocks will be seen, and Grande Galère, Bigorne and Sablonière may form a continuous line (see photo). It is then advisable when approaching Marmotière to keep the black panels open to the right of the flagstaff as the tip of the reef that extends north of Maître Ile abuts the transit (see plan).

Anchorage

If it has been replaced, deep-draught yachts should anchor or moor to the States buoy. The States buoy was removed in 1995 and there were four private moorings in position, leaving little room to anchor out of the stream which runs strongly east of the island. If vacant and sufficiently strong, a private mooring may be borrowed, but not at weekends.

There are half-tide private moorings and a States mooring on sand to the west of Marmotière but, on a rising tide when the shingle ridge joining Marmotière to Blanche covers, the current sweeps round the island and yachts taking off, depending on draught, may swing into those still aground.

After inspecting the area at low water, those that can take the ground may proceed into

Looking W from Marmotière at LW

Marmotière from Blanche I. at HW neaps

Marmotière from the west near LW

the pool, preferably by skirting Marmotière through the drying moorings, or perhaps by using the 'Suez Canal' (see photo E03 (page 116) taken at LWS).

The drying areas have extensive deep ridges/ troughs and drying out cannot be recommended without a low-water inspection by dinghy.

There are no facilities on the island and houseowners bring their water and supplies with them.

Plateau des Minquiers

An unintentional close approach to the Minquiers (*Minkies* on Dumaresq's map of 1685 and currently thus pronounced) is a matter of concern to most yachtsmen. They are notorious for their strong tidal streams and hazardous rocks stretching 15M east-west and 9M north-south. However, in settled weather, with light winds and good visibility, a visit can be recommended. The approach to Maîtresse Ile from the north is not difficult. Departure to the southeast, as long as the line is held accurately, is also possible, but the charted southern channel must be used, for entry or departure, with great caution and preferably after inspection by dinghy at low water.

In the 18th century Maîtresse Ile and Puffin were joined by a ridge, providing shelter for privateers, and the Royal Navy blasted or quarried it away. Later quarrymen built and lived in the huts on Maîtresse Ile that are now used, as in Les Ecrehou, by Jersey yachtsmen.

By 1800 the quarrymen, hacking stone for Fort Regent, had had enough and in 1807 they petitioned the Governor of Jersey to let them stop before they were swept away. He refused so they left for Chausey to work for the French.

For centuries French and Jersey fishermen shared the harvest of the Minquiers. Victor Hugo wrote about them in *The Toilers of the Sea*, and Hammond Innes' novel *The Wreck of the Mary Deare* is set there. In 1946, when the sovereignty of the reef was in dispute between France and England, the editor's uncle, retired from the Navy, was offered the post of sitting in the Minquiers with a shot gun to keep the French away. After considering the living conditions on Maîtresse Ile and the effective range of a shot gun, he wisely refused.

At the Hague in 1953 France lost her claim and removed all her magnificent buoys with their old names, Brisants du Sud, Caux and Les Sauvages. Since then, with the help of Trinity House, the States of Jersey have maintained an excellent buoyage system around the reef, installing the SW Minquiers etc.

Chart

Admiralty *3656* or the old Admiralty *2100* if obtainable.

Tidal levels referred to chart datum

48°58'N 2°08'W MHWS 11·6m MHWN 8·9m
MLWN 4·0m MLWS 1·4m MTL 6·5m

Tidal streams referred to HW St Helier

One mile north of Demie de Vascelin starboard buoy, marking the entrance to the northern approach channel to Maîtresse Ile:

HW−6, W 1·7–0·7 then slack and turning anticlockwise to:
HW−5, SE 0·4–0·2 increasing to:
HW−3, ESE 5·0–2·0 then decreasing to:
HW E 0·4–0·2 slackening and turning anticlockwise to:
HW+2 WNW 2·3–1·1 with a maximum:
HW+4 WNW 4·0–1·5

The stream runs SSE and NNW down the channel passing west of Maîtresse Ile with a maximum of 3½ knots SSE at HW−4 and 3 knots NNW at HW+2.

Northeast of Maîtresse Ile it can attain 7 knots through the Gouliot Passage.

South of the S Minquiers and SE Minquiers buoys the stream runs E or SE from HW−5 to HW St Helier with a maximum of 5 knots at springs and W or NW from HW+1 to HW−6 with a maximum of 4·7 knots at springs.

Depths

The anchorage in the pool south of Maîtresse Ile dries 1·2m but can be approached at half tide from the main channel over the sandbank south of *Les Demics*, which dries 4·2m (1995), or by the southeastern approach.

It is possible to remain afloat at anchor at all states of the tide in the main channel and in the anchorage north of the *Puffin* Beacon.

For a first brief visit, at neaps with an afternoon highwater, approaching from the north, the advice is to arrive at ½ flood. This will give three hours ashore before leaving at HW.

The anchorage in the south pool may however be subject to swell as the ridge between Maîtresse and La Grande Gouliot rock will cover at half tide.

Between highwater and half tide down the northerly stream over the ridge will be strong, especially at springs and there is the danger of being swept away when attempting to land by dinghy. Also, approaching from the north on a high tide, the top of the Jetée des Fontaines beacon will be inconspicuous and may even be covered!

For a longer visit, but only when familiar with the marks, approach from the north aiming to arrive (with due caution on a falling tide) just before half tide down when, at springs, most of the day may be spent ashore and you can investigate the southern entrance at LW. Entry at neaps may be less traumatic but, with an afternoon high water you will not have the shelter of the wide expanse of rocks, and the dangers of the southern passage will not be exposed.

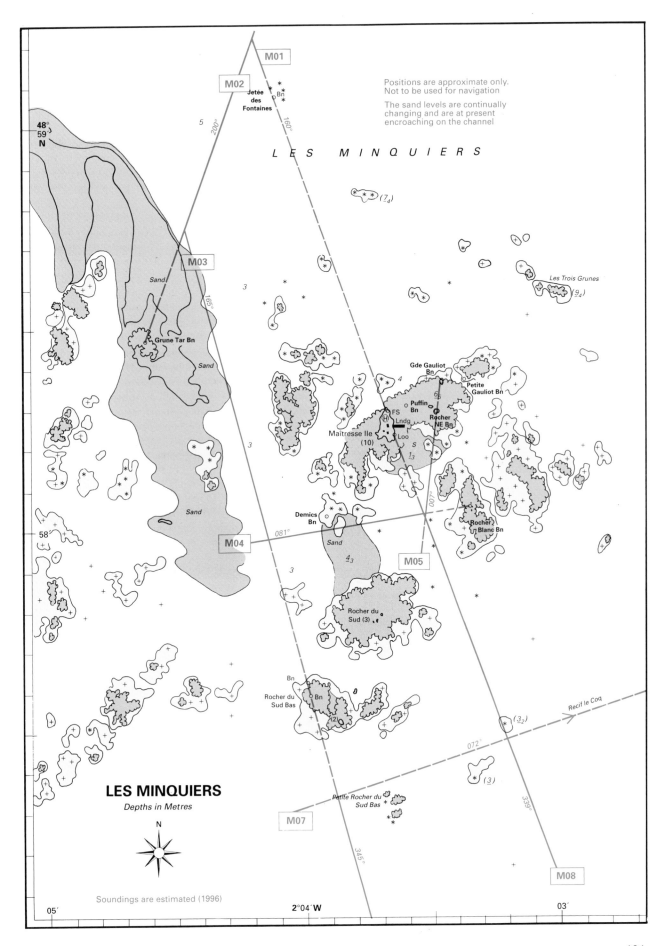

LES MINQUIERS

Positions are approximate only.
Not to be used for navigation

The sand levels are continually
changing and are at present
encroaching on the channel

L E S   M I N Q U I E R S

Jetée
des
Fontaines
Bn

Grune Tar Bn

Sand

Sand

Sand

Les Trois Grunes
(9_4)

(7_4)

Gde Gauliot
Bn

Petite
Gauliot Bn

Puffin
Bn

Rocher
NE Bn

FS

Lndg

Loo

Maîtresse Ile
(10)

1_3

Rocher
Blanc Bn

Demics
Bn

Sand

4_3

Rocher du
Sud (3)

Recif le Coq

(3_2)

Bn

Rocher du
Sud Bas

Bn

(2)

(3)

Petite Rocher du
Sud Bas

LES MINQUIERS

Depths in Metres

N

M01

M02

M03

M04

M05

M07

M08

Soundings are estimated (1996)

2°04'W

05'

03'

NORTHERN APPROACH (Grade EC)

The 10-mile passage from St Helier to the Demie de Vascelin, green unlit buoy with a radar echo-enhancer, is free of dangers and departure is marked by the power station chimney x Demie de Pas Lt on 255°. On sighting the buoy, with due allowance for the tidal stream, steer to leave it close to starboard while searching for the first marks:

Transit M01 160° – Jetée des Fontaines de Bas RW Bn x Maîtresse Ile Flagstaff (sectioned in black/white bands on the lower half). At weekends a resident will fly the Union flag, making the flagstaff easier to identify.

When 200m from the beacon alter to starboard onto:

Mark M02 200° – Grune Tar Bn, a white column with a 'T' topmark.

Hold Grune Tar on this bearing until:

Transit M03 165° – Rocher du Sud Bas beacons, only 15m apart, are in transit. The northern beacon is a pole with two red balls as a topmark and the south beacon is a white concrete column.

The sandbank running down the west side of the channel is encroaching so hold this transit with care until, leaving Les Demics (or Demies on the new charts) Bn pole with white 'D' topmark to port:

Transit M04 081° – the pole with cross topmark on Rocher Blanc is over the white painted patch on the rock, in front of which there is a small white pole with a red top.

Les Demics (Demies)   Rocher Blanc

M03

At half tide it is possible to turn to port onto this transit to pass over the rocky patch on the north end of the drying sandbank joining Les Demies to the Rocher du Sud (see plan). Steer on this transit until the slipway is well open and then turn north on:

Puffin I   States buoy   Gde Gauliot   Rocher NE   Petite Gauliot

Transit M05 007° – The Rocher NE RW Bn is in transit with La Grande Gauliot Bn pole, with a somewhat deformed open diamond looking like a bent ring as topmark, behind it and steer for the States buoy in the anchorage.

Anchorages

The drying anchorage is just south and west of the States buoy. The bottom is soft sand and mud with some rocky patches further east. A slipway leads up to the huts.

Photo M06 shows the anchorage with the black/ white toilet, the Loo, to the left of the yacht's mast.

M06

If there is not enough water to pass over the bank, anchor on soundings in the channel just southwest of the Demies or Demics Bn, west of the sand bar.

On a second visit it might be convenient to remain afloat north of the island 100m off Puffin beacon, black/white vertical stripes with a red square topmark. To reach this anchorage from the north, round the Jetée des Fontaines de Bas beacon, leaving it to port and steer 151°, with due attention to the tidal stream, on a line between Puffin Bn and Jetée des Fontaines de Bas Bn (astern on the reciprocal 331°). This course leaves the Jetée des Fontaines rocks, drying 7·4m close to port and a rock drying 1·8m close to starboard.

Many Channel Islanders prefer to pass round the island by the eastern Petite Gauliot Passage, but this should not be attempted by strangers without an experienced Jerseyman on board.

SOUTHERN APPROACH (Grade EC to H)

This entry is not easy and should not be attempted without first using it for departure, after identifying the dangers at low water as the plan cannot be relied upon in this area.

Entering from the south, leave the SE Minquiers E card buoy 1M to starboard and steer for Maîtresse Ile on 342°. In excellent visibility, St Peter's church spire, St Helier, will be in transit with the island.

From a distance of 2M identify the leading beacons on Rocher de Sud Bas (see photo M03, viewed from the north). With the beacons in line steer 345° and identify Recif Le Coq Bn, a RW pole with heavy wire guys, 2M to starboard.

Hold the transit of 345° until:

Breast mark M07 072° – Recif Le Coq Bn is just open to the north of the Petit Rocher du Sud Bas rocks.

From this point a possible course might be to steer to make good 275° and when the huts on Maîtresse Ile are open to the west of the northernmost Rocher du Sud Bas Bn, steer a northerly course (approximately 010°), with due allowance for tide, leaving the Rocher du Sud Bas beacons 100–200m to starboard.

This is the most difficult part of the passage as there are heads to the southwest of Rocher du Sud to be left to starboard. Past the two beacons steer a northwesterly course until the flagstaff on Maîtresse Ile is open to the west of Les Demies (Demics) Bn. Steer along this line until the Rocher de Sud Bas beacons are in transit on 165°. A turn to starboard may then be made to cross the sandbank and enter the southern anchorage with the Rocher Blanc beacons in transit on 081°.

SOUTHEAST APPROACH (Grade EC)

If there is 4m or more at the States buoy it is possible to *leave* by this passage on a single transit. The marks are hard to identify from a distance and entry should only be attempted when thoroughly familiar with the area.

There is a toilet on Maîtresse Ile, the Loo, which is painted on the south side with black/white bands (see photo below).

The lower half of the flagstaff is also painted with black/white bands.

Photo Justine Coom

Transit M08 339° – The transit is with the flagstaff x the Loo on 339°. Leave with this as a stern transit and hold it accurately for at least 2M with due allowance for the tidal stream.

Facilities

Except for the Loo there are no facilities on the island and visitors must bring their own water and supplies with them.

Looking NW over the anchorage near LW

Looking NE over the Rocher du Sud Bas beacons

Looking NW over the Rocher Blanc Beacon near HW *Photo* Peter Carnegie

Tidal streams

Arrows show direction.
Figures show the rates of flow in knots at neaps
followed by springs

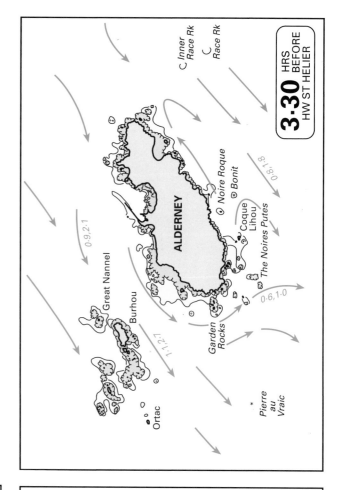

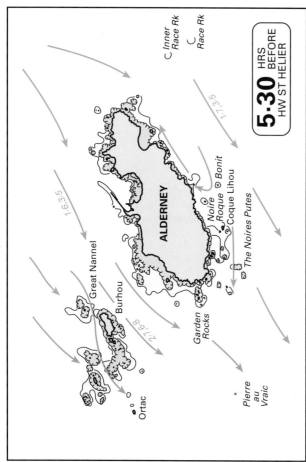

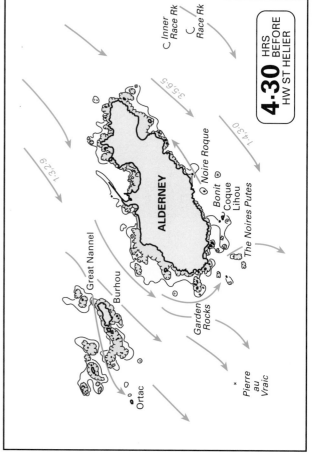

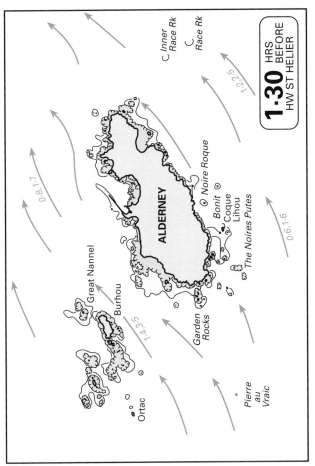

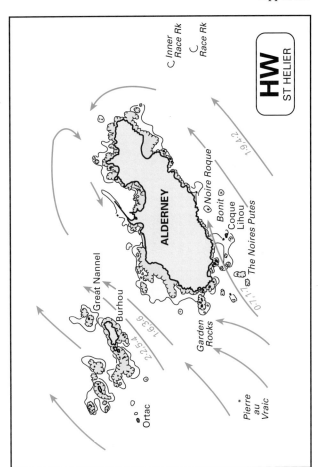

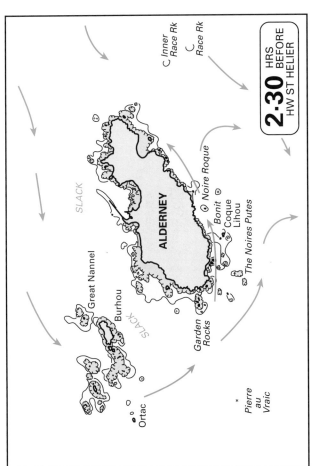

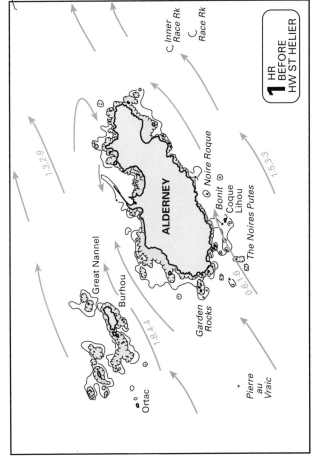

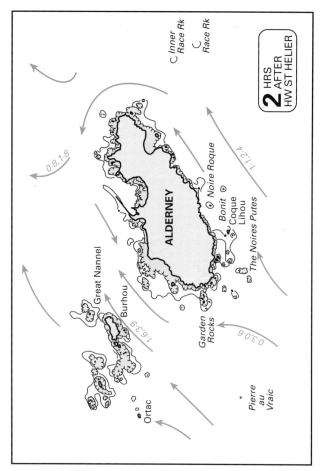

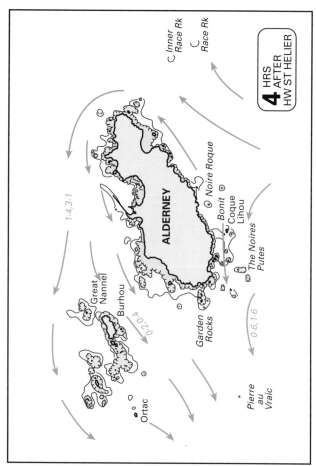

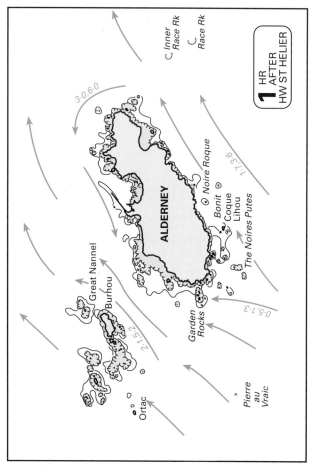

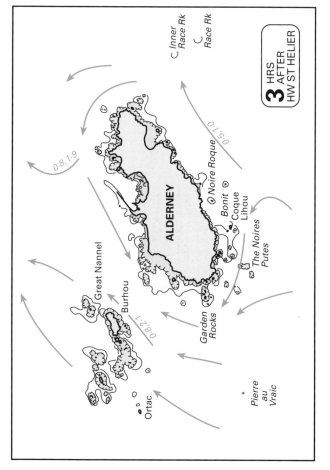

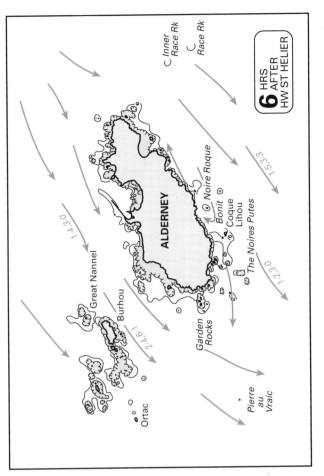

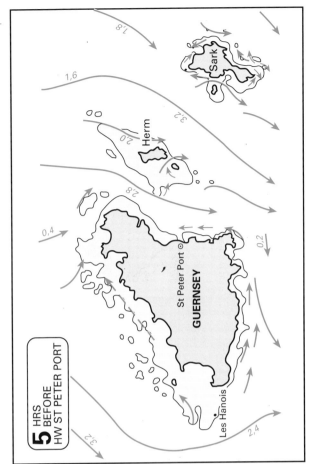

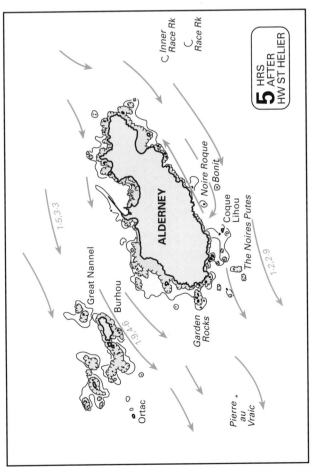

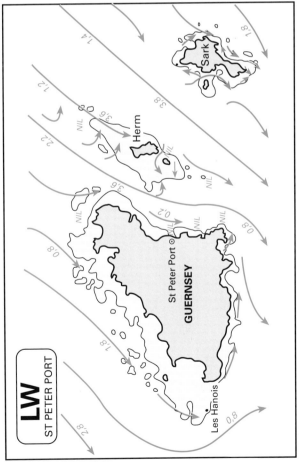

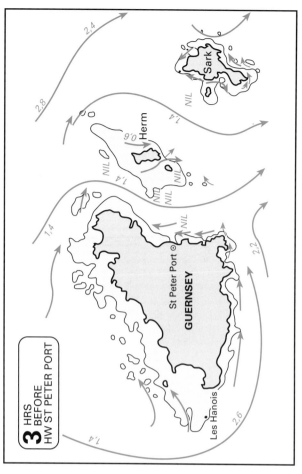

3 HRS BEFORE HW ST PETER PORT

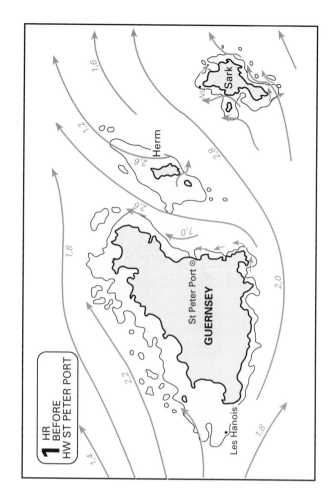

1 HR BEFORE HW ST PETER PORT

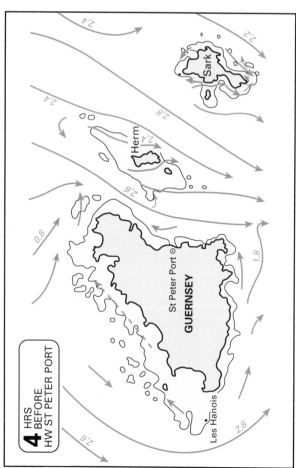

4 HRS BEFORE HW ST PETER PORT

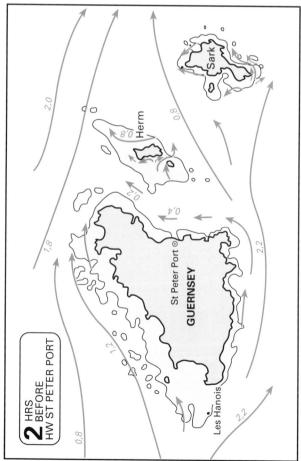

2 HRS BEFORE HW ST PETER PORT

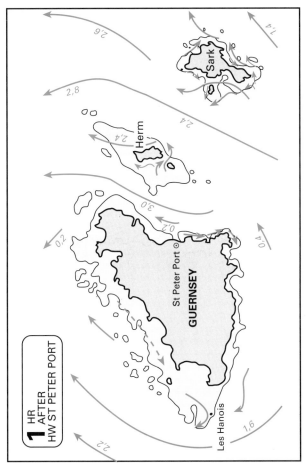

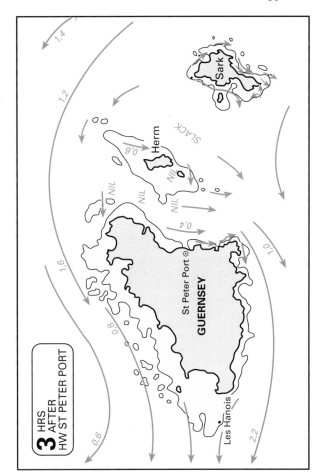

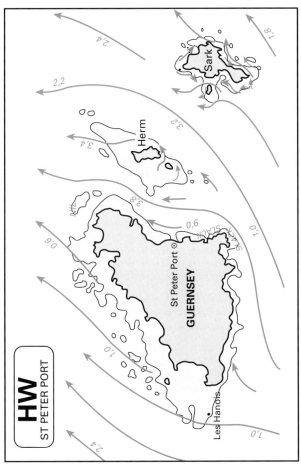

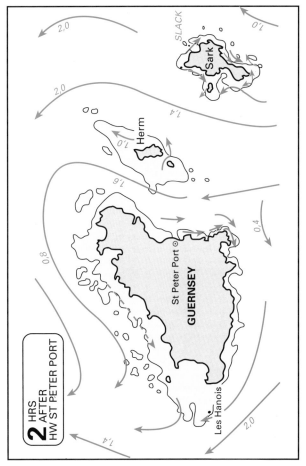

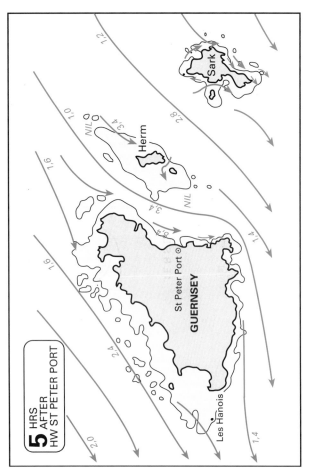

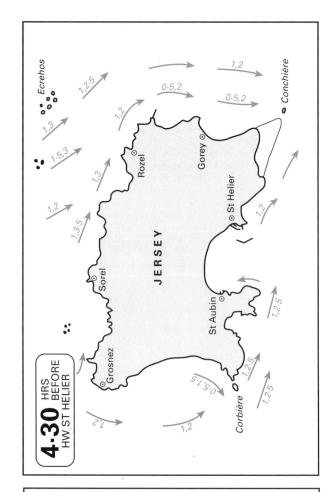

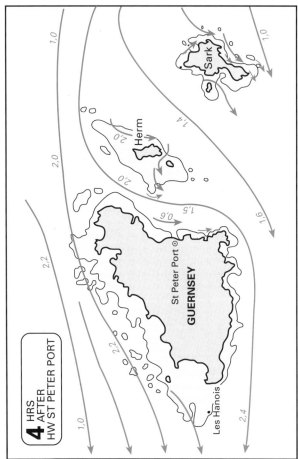

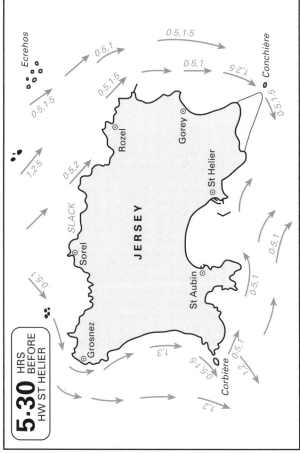

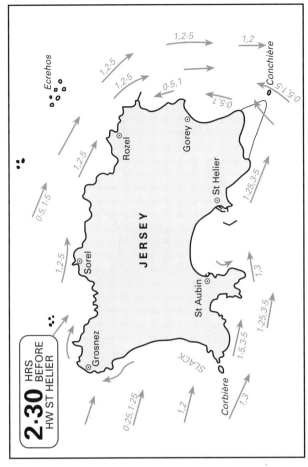

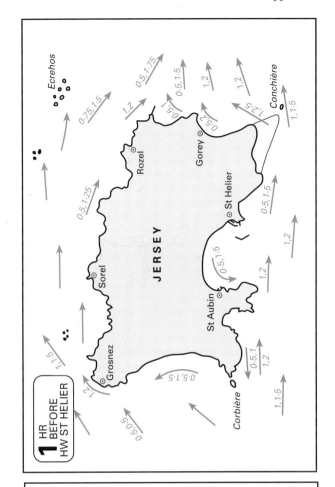

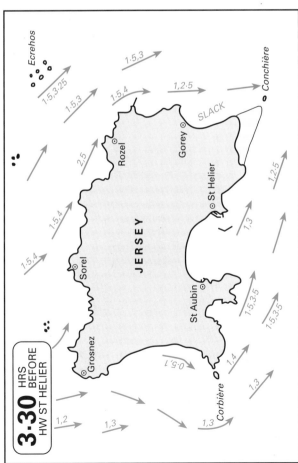

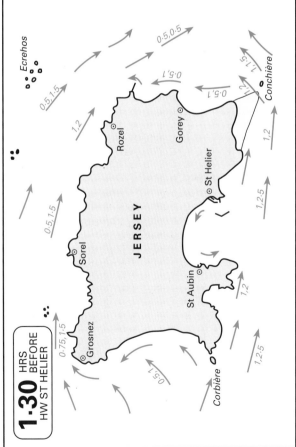

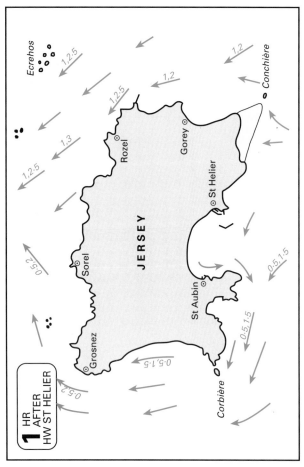

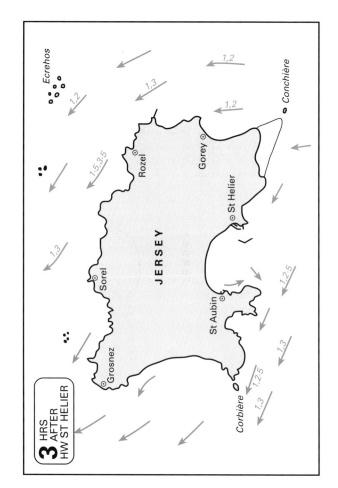

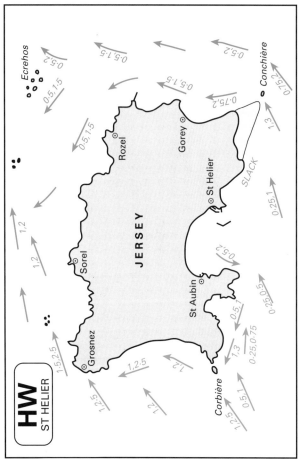

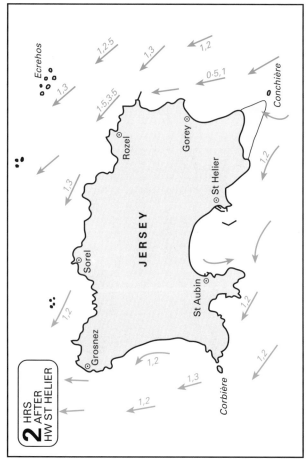

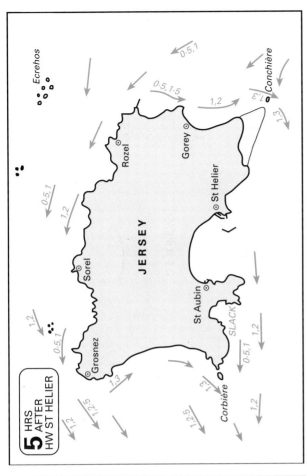

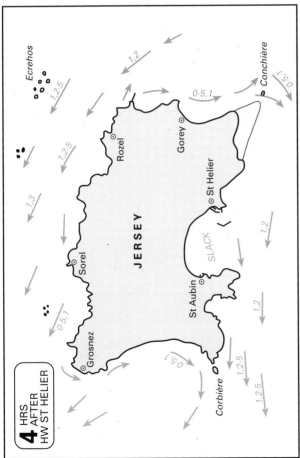

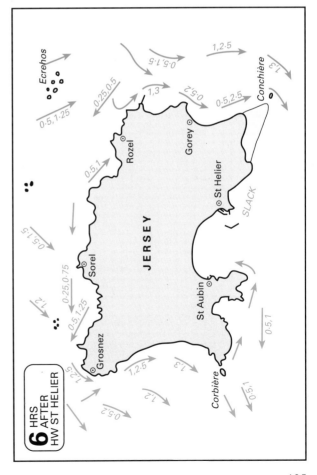

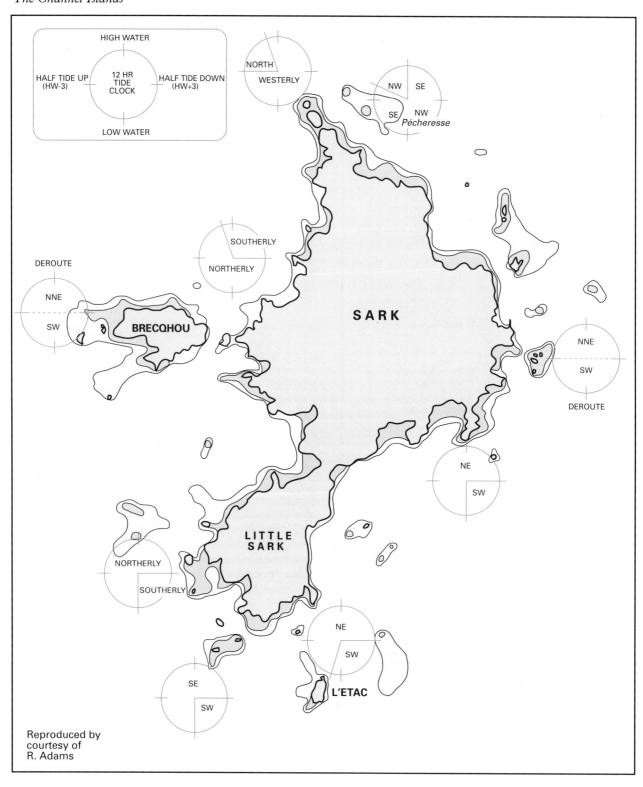

Reproduced by
courtesy of
R. Adams

The 12-hour clocks show the general direction of the tidal stream at various positions round Sark.
The DEROUTE clocks are for the stream clear west and east of Sark (i.e off the plan).
Example - At The Pécheresse the stream runs SE from HW to HW+3, then NW from HW+3 to HW+6, SE again from HW+6 to
HW−2 and finally NW from HW−2 to HW.

Index